HOW TO AVOID THE 10 MISTAKES SINGLE Women MAKE

Michelle McKinney Hammond

HARVEST HOUSE PUBLISHERS
EUGENE, OREGON

Published in association with the literary agency of Alive Literary Agency, 7680 Goddard Street, Ste #200, Colorado Springs, CO 80920. www.alivecommunications.com.

Cover by Franke Design and Illustration, Excelsior, Minnesota

HOW TO AVOID THE 10 MISTAKES SINGLE WOMEN MAKE
Copyright © 2006 by Michelle McKinney Hammond
Published 2015 by Harvest House Publishers
Eugene, Oregon 97402
www.harvesthousepublishers.com

ISBN 978-0-7369-6335-0 (pbk.)
ISBN 978-0-7369-6336-7 (eBook)

Library of Congress Cataloging-in-Publication Data

McKinney Hammond, Michelle.
  How to avoid the 10 mistakes single women make / Michelle McKinney Hammond
    p. cm.
  ISBN 978-0-7369-1391-1 (pbk.)
  1. Single women—Religious life. 2. Christian women—Religious life. I. Title.
  BV4596.S5M3445 2006
  248.8'432—dc22
                    2006007137

Printed in the United States of America

15 16 17 18 19 20 21 22 23 / BP-JH / 10 9 8 7 6 5 4 3 2 1

This is to all my sisters who struggle on the first day of spring, through many a lonely night while whispering prayers in the dark, and with every tick of the clock that grows louder on the mantel of your heart. Have hope your prince will come.

In the meantime occupy well, look your best, and know that you are not alone.

Acknowledgments

To my Harvest House family, who continually encourages and inspires me to greater heights.

To all those who support, counsel, pray, and challenge me to do better, thank you.

But most of all, to those whose needs cause me to seek God for even more answers on your behalf. It is my constant privilege to serve you.

Contents

A unique top ten list

Hmm…let's see…

David Letterman had them. *USA Today.* MTV. *Billboard.* *The New York Times.* Anybody who is anybody has a top ten list for this or that. Most of these lists are cute, funny, and quite entertaining. But, though they clue us in on the state of mind of the general masses, they really have nothing to do with our personal lives. Perhaps it's time we make a few lists of our own. It's called taking stock. Locating ourselves. Where we are at present in comparison to where we really want to be. In order to move forward and reach our personal goals, we must acknowledge the stuff, the issues, the habits, and the mind-sets that keep us stuck and hinder our progress.

It's safe to say that most singles want to be married, and yet they are at a loss to figure out what may be stalling their advancement toward the altar. As I have traveled around the country, speaking and corresponding with singles from around the world, certain patterns have emerged and common threads of conversation and behavior have made me pause for the cause and devise a top ten list of my own. Ten mistakes singles make in their pursuit of love, romance, and personal fulfillment.

I hope you will be brave enough to be honest with yourself, examine your baggage, and get rid of what is not working for you. That is, if you are serious about changing your circumstances. Of course, it all begins with renewing the mind, so let's walk through this together. Know this: You are not alone, and there is never any shame in making a mistake. It's only a shame if you don't learn from your faux pas. So here's to living, learning, and rounding the bend to a place in the journey of life where you enjoy the scenery much more and finally arrive at your desired destination. Just remember that you are the driver behind the wheel and this is your car. You get to decide where you want to go, so check the map and adjust your route accordingly.

As always with love,

Michelle

*Placing marriage on
a pedestal next to God*

Just thinking out loud...

Once upon a time a young man longed to be free from the things that bound him. Feelings of inferiority, isolation, and helplessness overwhelmed him. But God had chosen him to be a conqueror, to defy the odds, to rise above mediocrity and literally free, not just himself from the oppression that hindered him from living the life he wanted to live, but also the lives of countless others around him.

But how would he do this? First, he had to get past what he had always believed about himself. His description of himself did not match God's description. God called him a mighty man of valor. He saw himself as insignificant, the least among men, someone not to be taken note of. He was amazed to find he did not realize his own power or the power of the God he served to grant him his heart's desire. Neither had he considered the fact that God was with him and actually interested in his state of affairs. That God wanted him to live a victorious life.

These were truths he had to embrace in order to be empowered to take the next step toward living the bold and victorious life he was longing to live. He had to cast down his own perceptions about himself and embrace the true reality of who he was in the eyes of the One who had created him and knew him best.

He had to acknowledge all of his weaknesses, strengths, and even those things he was just beginning to discover about himself.

It is only when we locate ourselves that we are able to get a vision of our destiny and what we can accomplish. When we come to the full realization of our inherent gifts and the things in our nature that are conducive to God's design for our lives, we can see the road map and make sense of the directions God is giving us. Of course, there are seasons when we are called to walk by faith, taking one step at a time into what *seems* to be the dark. But in those times we are held safe in the center of God's palm all the way. So remember, when you can't see your way, it's because you are being held. And when you can see the path before you, keep moving forward, being sensitive to His voice every step of the way. How often have you said to yourself, "Something told me…" and then ignored the instructions because you thought it was just you second-guessing yourself? That is not some*thing;* that is Some*one* whispering, "This is the way, walk in it…" (Isaiah 30:21). As we learn to trust that voice and follow His instructions, we find ourselves on the path of wholeness and living the life we desire with less drama and trauma than when we plot our course ourselves.

Know that getting your dream will always cost you something. We can only hold on to so much collectively in our lives. Often, something has to go in order to be replaced by something better. This is why the Bible tells us that we cannot serve two masters at the same time. We will love one and hate the other (Matthew 6:24; Luke 16:13). If you truly want to be married, there are things about the single life you will have to sacrifice. Life can no longer be as self-centered; it must become others-centered. The focus you once had on yourself must now be shifted to invest in the life or lives of someone else. When we are seeking to establish a covenant with God or someone in our life, we must be willing to sacrifice anything that would hinder the relationship from moving forward toward a rich commitment in which both people experience the blessing of pouring themselves into one another's lives.

Back to our young man. After getting a clear understanding of who he really was, it was time to make a sacrifice. He had to build an altar to God, establishing a covenant with Him as well as affirming that it was He who gave him peace in the midst of his turmoil within and without.

After this he had to get rid of some idols. They were hindering his ability to see the endless possibilities for his life. They were distracting his focus from the main point that in spite of what he thought he lacked—strength, wisdom, support, and courage—he served a God who was Lord over all the impossibilities he could list. Idols were robbing him of the life he wanted to live. They had become larger than God in his mind, obstructing his view of a better tomorrow.

After tearing down the idols, he was able to receive instructions from God that directed him on how to make his dream come true. Gideon then led his people to freedom from their oppressors through highly unconventional means. Along the way his faith was tested as God challenged him to let go of everything he assumed would get him the victory he wanted. (Read Gideon's story in Judges 6–8.)

Perhaps you too feel insignificant and isolated in your longing for victory in the arena of love. Feeling oppressed by the way that life has always been, you've grown accustomed to being disappointed. Friends reenforce what you already feel and offer no new hope. Weary from the struggle, you've decided that life is "just that way." That some lucky ones escape from the single zoo while you remain behind bars, peering through your longings for a love to call your own.

Perhaps you too have accepted a different view of yourself than what God has of you. While you are answering to the name "Undesirable," He is calling you "Beloved." Could it be that you need to make a sacrifice of your old ideals and reach out to the One who loves you most and discover the peace He brings, though nothing has changed yet? Perhaps you have a few idols of your own to shatter and displace from the lofty mantel in your heart—visions of how life should be and what it will take to make you happy. Perhaps old habits and mind-sets have kept you bound in patterns of behavior that invite defeat and disillusion-ment. God is calling you to think outside the box. To embrace a new way of thinking and living. To eliminate the things and people that hold you back from getting the victory you want in every area of your life, including love.

Change is never comfortable at first, but it is necessary if you want to alter the outcome you've been getting. It's time to use new muscles. To stretch, to grow, to even dare to experiment. How far will you go to get what you really want? How badly do you want it? If you are truly serious about getting the love you want, there is work to be done.

LET'S BEGIN WITH A PERSONAL ASSESSMENT

∝ How do you see yourself?

∝ How would you describe yourself to someone else?

∝ What mind-sets have you adopted about why you don't have the love you want?

∝ What insights have others given you? Are they valid?

∝ What are you willing to change in order to obtain different results?

Solution: Tear down the idols

Oops!

The word "oops" suggests something slipping out of one's grasp or one's control, or unexpectedly giving way and spilling, bruising, or breaking an object or a part of one's anatomy. It's an exclamation of surprise—part involuntary, part apologetic. It's a word that is as natural as breathing. It's uttered without a thought, an unconscious reaction to the occurrence. One does not deliberately allow something to fall, to shatter, or to be wasted. No, these incidences are usually followed by regret and an assessment if repairs can be made or if there is a need for a replacement.

That works for objects, not for life. Yet many singles find themselves somewhere along the journey of life voicing their dismay at their shattered expectations, broken heart, wounded self-esteem, and the fractured view of a life half lived as they wait for their "other half" to arrive and carry them to the land of wholeness, where all things are beautiful and perfect. Ha! This is the first mistake.

I am reminded of a conversation God had with Adam when he hid after eating the fruit from the tree of the knowledge of good and evil. Adam explained that he hid because he was naked, to which God replied, "Who told you that you were naked?"

(Genesis 3:11). Good question. Adam and Eve had been naked and unashamed, unaware that anything was missing from their lives until someone else introduced a different way of looking at their circumstances. All of a sudden the very thing they had been able to freely celebrate became an issue that clouded the beauty of their pleasurable experience in the garden as something that was shameful.

How many times does a perfectly pleasant family gathering get ruined by all too familiar words from some concerned, well-meaning family member or friend? "So why aren't you married yet?" "Perhaps you are too picky." All of a sudden you find yourself questioning your marketability as a "good catch." You begin to wonder, *What is wrong with me?* You, like Adam and Eve, begin to feel naked. Ashamed, vulnerable, and insufficiently equipped for the journey of life because all of a sudden you are made to feel like part of a motley minority. Which by the way is not true. When you consider the rising number of singles between never married, divorced and widowed people, you're not so weird after all!

Of course, if you don't know this, the deeper you will drift into the depths of uncertainty about the worth of your heart, your love, and your presence not only in the life of someone who should appreciate it immensely, but your very existence on the planet! Something else kicks in. It's the internal pressure that says you need someone in order for you to have any sense of validation or affirmation that you are indeed *not* naked. That you *are* loveable. Desirable. All that and a bag of chips. A worthy entity in the earth realm, you must have someone in your life to stamp you fully dressed. Perhaps if we are honest with ourselves, we would have to admit that at times the shame of being a lone ranger escalates our desire for a mate above the more qualitative reasons for wanting one, such as wanting to be a blessing to someone, a life partner, a coconspirator…come on, you know what I'm talkin' about! There are right reasons and wrong reasons for desiring marriage. This brings to light the fact that you must have a sense of your own personal value before you can expect someone else to recognize it. Talk about putting the cart before the horse if you are expecting someone to lend you self-worth! It simply won't happen. Why not, you ask?

First, God will never allow another person to be your affirmation and completion. This is a job He has reserved for Himself. If someone was able to complete you, there would be no need for Him. This is something He will not stand for. Second, the person who could add all that you're looking for to your life is also looking for someone who can add something to his life. Another person who has nothing to bring to the party but her need for validation will not be an attractive package. Therefore, your only choice would be someone who is as needy as yourself. Not a pretty picture, and certainly not the makings of a healthy relationship.

Now, let's see what else could be making you feel less lovable and less desirable than the average bear. The media doesn't help. Everyone is in love in the movies. Love always triumphs and people live happily ever after in Technicolor—or should I say high-definition glory? If seeing is believing, then we will buy into the lie that the norm in society is an oo-some twosome, and yet, generally speaking, most singles in the real world struggle to find real role models of marital bliss. Between peer pressure and media pressure, most people end up marrying for the wrong reasons to the wrong people and find themselves with greater problems than the average single on any given day. Could it be that buying the lie that marriage is the end all, be all and the completion of all things worth mentioning has caused us to erect false idols that keep us in bondage to unfulfillment and unhappiness?

This being the case, how does one realign her thought life to a healthier and more balanced way of viewing the infinite possibilities that life holds, no matter what her romantic status? If you are tussling with God over the idol of marriage, it's bound to have a jolting end. Somewhere along the way the idol will slip through your fingers, come crashing to the ground, and shatter into a million unretrievable pieces. It's called coming to the end of yourself. Where all your preconceived notions of the life you had envisioned for yourself must be put to rest before you can open your arms to embrace the life God has for you in the present, as well as anticipate amazing surprises that will bring indescribable joy to you in the future.

Go ahead and take a deep breath. Open your heart as well as your hands and repeat after me: "Life does not consist of those who make me feel that I count. It consists of how much value I add to the life of others." At the end of the day, the things that will make you feel the richest are the lives of those you affect for the good. Your worth through God's eyes has already been determined. In His mind you are priceless. There is nothing on earth that can match your worth; therefore, the price for you had to be paid by heavenly means. Jesus literally had to leave heaven and enter the earth through the womb of a woman in order to pay a price that would be acceptable to God to redeem you. Now you have the awesome responsibility of redeeming your worth here on earth by glorifying God whether you are married or not.

Your worth will never be measured by whom you attract, but rather by whom you affect and how you affect them. Whether someone chooses you or not does not determine your worth. If you go to the store and decide you don't want to pay for something because the price is too high, the salesclerk does not lower the price to what you think is acceptable. If the clerk is really good, she will point you in the direction of things that fit your budget and leave the more expensive fare for someone who is willing to pay the price! Your value can never be estimated based on how others feel about you.

The goal of life must change in order for the idol to be destroyed. No longer should your self-worth hang in the balance on the technicality of the interest of others. You were created on purpose to be a life-changing instrument to all you encounter. The atmosphere should change when you walk into the room. You should be a walking conduit of light and life—God's light and the life that comes from walking in His Word, because that is truly what life consists of. "Man shall not live by bread alone, but by every word that proceeds from the mouth of God" (Matthew 4:4 NKJV).

Our lives are transformed by the renewing of our minds (Romans 12:2); therefore, a new mind-set needs to be adopted in order to keep the voices of the idols from drowning out the truth of God's Word for our lives. The promises of God are where our assurance, validation, and fulfillment must come from. His promises include His view of you as a valuable addition to the citizenry of the world—someone who is vital, alive, and full of purpose. This is the place where being single can work for you. It is only your attitude that will work against you, so choose to master it.

What should you know that will set you on the path of wholeness as a single person?

First, settle the issue that it is fine to desire a mate. This is a natural, God-given desire. Note that there is a difference between *you* having a desire and *your desire having you*. God created you to be in control—not just in the spiritual realm, but also in the natural. This was the first assignment for the man and the woman when they were placed in the Garden of Eden. "Eden" means "pleasure," yet God expected them to exercise control in order to maintain the pleasure He instituted. He handed the reins to us to be master of our flesh, our emotions, and our desires. To subdue anything that might try to overtake or overwhelm us. We, therefore, have been empowered to have dominion over our flesh and anything that might rob us of our focus or distract us away from living the life God intended us to live. One filled with pleasure and fulfillment.

Second, you should know there is no formula for happiness and fulfillment. Marriage, riches, fame—nothing can fill the spot that only God can fill. Don't believe the hype or get distracted by counterfeit joy.

Third, there is a time and purpose for every season under heaven, and seasons do change. Make the most of your present; it will ultimately affect your future.

Fourth, your marriage will only be as successful as your single life. Nurture wholeness where you are. The more you bring to the party, the greater a celebration it will be when others join you. All this and more as we walk through this thing together.

GETTING REAL

ᐟ᙮ What are three things you can't live without?

ᐟ᙮ Are you living without these things at present?

ᐟ᙮ How does their absence affect the quality of your life?

ᐟ᙮ What can you do to flourish in spite of what you presently lack?

Those who cling to worthless idols forfeit

the grace that could be theirs.

JONAH,
after some very uncomfortable days
spent in the belly of a fish.

Using singleness as an excuse to not getting on with the incredible business of living

Just thinking out loud...

He lay there in the dirt by the road, paralyzed but praying and hoping for a miracle. Then a stranger was standing in front of him, asking a question that seemed to be obvious: "Do you want to be whole?" It was a good question. One he had not considered. He knew he no longer wanted to be where he was, but he had grown certain that things would never change. His friends and acquaintances seconded the motion, which was not surprising, since they were no better off than he was. After all, misery loves company. They couldn't see beyond where they were, had trouble moving forward in their own lives, or were simply marking time as well. Stuck on stupid, stuck on past pain, stuck on wrong attitudes—there were a plethora of reasons for why, but the bottom line was the same for them all across the board. They were stuck. They had settled on excuses that removed them from the responsibility of living and overcoming. It was someone else's fault that they were broken, fractured, empty...not whole.

She had grown used to life the way it was, though it went against every principle and value she possessed. She went along with the status quo, remaining silent when she probably should have spoken up, feeling outnumbered. She was the one trying to live right. Do the right thing. Live a godly life amid a society that allowed their flesh and desires to dominate their discipline. She was embarrassed by the conversations she overheard of things done in secret that should have remained there. And even though she knew it was against her better judgment, she wondered if she was crazy for trying to maintain a standard of purity. *Why bother?* she thought. *Everyone else is doing what they please and seeming to get away with it. They are enjoying life, and I am standing on the fringes looking in, missing out on all the fun.*

Every day she felt the pull of temptation on her flesh more and more. She had been swept away by their lifestyle before finding herself held captive by its intoxicating blend of things that titillated the senses. She had been rescued and restored back to safety, only to find the way of the world slowly wooing her once more. Though she knew better, it was hard to resist its pull. She was torn between two lovers, the spirit and the flesh, warring for her soul. Slowly, and without any discernable movement, compromise began to sneak into her conversation and outlook. She could feel herself teetering on the brink of temptations too shameful to mention. But before she fell into the deep end of the pool of her desires, two visitors arrived, snatching her back to sharp awareness that to continue in this state would be dangerous. She and her family needed to leave. To separate themselves from an atmosphere that was most definitely penetrating their front door, coming to roost in the center of their home. She knew it was the best thing to do, but perhaps she had lingered too long, listening to their conversation, coveting their "freedom." Though her feet led her one way, her heart was divided—fascinated with the decadence she intellectually abhorred but secretly yearned to experience.

In midflight she looked back to catch one last glimpse of what could have been if she had only been able to let herself go. And that is when she got stuck. Stuck on the past. Stuck on her past mistakes. Stuck on the things she thought she had missed. She coveted the lifestyle of those who did as they pleased and didn't comprehend the safety of the boundaries that God had set for her. She couldn't go back, and she couldn't move forward. What if…what if…what if…

What if you didn't blame anyone else for where you are and took ownership of your own life? How powerful would that be? What if you could move beyond your past mistakes and experiences? What if you didn't allow your standards to be clouded by the blindness of others? If you did not covet that which is deceptively attractive but destructive to the heart and soul? Unfortunately she, being Lot's wife, did not have the advantage of having a conversation with Jesus like the paralyzed man (Genesis 19; John 5).

Could it be that you too suffer from paralysis? Being limited and devoid of ambition has become a way of life—your normal. The enemy of your soul, along with your friends, has seconded the motion that *this is as good as it gets. Don't you dare hope for anything better or different.* Remember, misery loves company. One thing is sure—both of those people suffered from the influence of their environment.

Society can play tricks that cause you to war against yourself and your better judgment. Friends can be placating because of their own weaknesses, preferring that you not magnify their failures by overcoming your own. Inevitably, the results are the same—you find yourself stuck. Longing for something different yet seduced by the familiar, we all are tempted to stay where we are because the unknown on the other side of where we want to be, though attractive, can also be scary. It's a lonely walk when you decide to strike out against all odds. Dare to break your pattern. Do something different or unusual. Sometimes you have to talk to yourself if you're the only person listening.

Swimming upstream is rough, yet Jesus, the friend who sticks closer than a brother, did not have time to attend a pity party with this man who had been lying in the same spot for 38 years, waiting for something different to happen. He gave him a very simple command. "Get up! Pick up your mat and walk" (John 5:8). Which the man, I'm sure to his own surprise, promptly did. Without a hand out or an arm up. Without assistance. Of his own volition and will, he was on his feet. All it took was a decision. A decision to do something different.

In contrast, even though Lot's wife looked as if she were moving in the right direction, she allowed her heart to betray her. It takes more than a decision to get what you want out of life. You must now be committed to the decision. There will always be room for questioning if you are making the right move. No movement can occur until every part of your will lines up with the direction you want to move in. Several Scriptures come to mind. "Any kingdom divided against itself will be ruined, and a house divided against itself will fall" (Luke 11:17). How could anything continue to stand if it is imploding? "No one who puts his hand to the plow and looks back is fit for service in the kingdom" (Luke 9:62). Or marriage or anything that requires a full-on commitment in order to work. Or check this one out: "If any of you lacks wisdom, [she] should ask God, who gives generously to all without finding fault, and it will be given to [her]. But when [she] asks, [she] must believe and not doubt, because [she] who doubts is like a wave of the sea, blown and tossed by the wind. That [woman] should not think [she] will receive anything from the Lord; [she] is a double-minded [woman], unstable in all [she] does" (James 1:5-8). Wow! Even God wants you to make up your mind.

Can you imagine Him answering one of your prayers and having you switch your desire in midstream? God will not be reduced to an errand boy for an indecisive master. And so He waits. He waits for you not only to become clear about your desire, but also to line up that desire with where He wants to take you in order for you to walk into the fullness of the blessings He has prepared for you. What are you waiting for?

LET'S TAKE STOCK OF WHERE YOU ARE

ᴄₑ What dreams have not been realized in your life?

ᴄₑ What mind-sets keep you trapped in your present way of living?

ᴄₑ What things in your environment keep you from seeing a way out of your present circumstances?

ᴄₑ What do you think you need in order to experience a personal breakthrough?

ᴄₑ What can you do to break your "normal" pattern of life?

Solution: Take your life off hold

"I'm bored!" Well, whose fault is that? The only people interested in entertaining you are those who get paid for it; otherwise, you are pretty much on your own. Life is a party you create; don't wait to be invited to one. I'm sure if we were on an episode of *Family Feud* with the question being what are some of the dumb things singles are guilty of, we would hear the host happily quip, "Survey says...They put their lives on hold!"

Even I have to put up a guilty finger on this one. Thank heaven this season of my life is over and I finally got a clue. The only thing that should be reserved for marriage is sex (but we'll talk about that later). Otherwise, it's time to let the games begin. Stop waiting for someone else to make your life happen. There is an endless world of possibilities for pleasure and fulfilling living at your fingertips. Fortunately, as a single person all your resources are yours to invest into living the life you want without having to check with anyone else. This makes for options and opportunities that are sure to be the envy of your married friends. There is no time like the present to enjoy what you might not be able to do tomorrow because of different priorities.

What does a no-holds-barred life look like? It's downright exciting. I repeatedly tell people I meet to finish this statement:

"I've always wanted to_____." Well, what's stopping you? Certainly your excuse should not be "Because I have no man." Until that blessed addition to your life shows up to claim you, your life should be full of fulfilling activities and amazing experiences that broaden you intellectually, emotionally, and spiritually as a person. In other words, get a life. Get one that will make you interesting and intriguing to others. A well-lived life full of passion and interests is like a magnet. It will draw other exciting people to you. So go ahead and mix it up.

First, break out of your regular routine. In order to have new experiences, you have to do new things. If your weekly routine is work, church, and back home, there is a lot of room for improvement. Select activities that interest you or pull you out of your comfort zone and stretch you. Remember, if you choose things that really interest you, chances are there will be other people there with the same interests, which make for fertile ground to meet your ideal mate. According to Dr. Neil Clark Warren, founder of eHarmony.com, the more things two people have in common, the greater their chances are of having a lasting relationship.

"Well, what kinds of things do you suggest, Michelle?" I suggest you experiment with anything that makes you curious; involves self-improvement; or adds to your skill sets, community involvement, or charitable ventures. Get active in areas you are concerned about. Check out an area which addresses what you feel you are lacking in your life. For instance, if the alarm on your biological clock is on full tilt sound off, why not consider mentoring children? Get involved with children's church or a youth program. Stop insisting on one way to have personal fulfillment and broaden your scope.

Take a class in an area of interest. From fun to educational, it's a great way to stretch beyond your present boundaries, increase your knowledge, and meet interesting people. Let me interject here that you might need to think outside of your religious box. A lot of us have a very unhealthy opinion of what holiness looks like, and holiness often ends up looking boring. I do not believe Jesus was boring by any stretch of the imagination. He was very social and always up for attending a good dinner, banquet, wedding, or celebration. His circle of friends and associates was an eclectic mix—from the very wealthy to the socially unacceptable. The Pharisees were appalled by the company He kept and the places He went. They accused Him of drinking and eating too much, but He had an interesting life, to say the least. The most unlikely people embraced Him and His teaching because of His friendly influence. Remember, your life has to look attractive in order for others to want to join you. You, like Jesus, will have to think outside of the religious box in order to have a life filled with excitement and fulfillment.

That being said, check your motives for why you do what you do and go where you go. Is it because you think you will meet the mate of your dreams or is it because you are truly interested in what that class or activity has to offer you personally? It should be all about you first. The motive should not be meeting someone. Trust me. Ruth was not thinking about meeting Boaz or any other man when she went gleaning. Her total focus was eating and surviving, and she still got a rich man out of the deal! (Ruth 2–4). Meeting someone should be the by-product of what you do, not the primary goal. In the meantime, get ready to expand your personal breadth as a person.

What other dreams do you have? What are some things you want to acquire? Don't wait for a man to come and buy you jewelry and trinkets; set a standard for them to follow. Acquire a nice piece that signals you are a woman of quality. I don't know about you, but holding out for my knight in shining armor to show up, marry me, and buy a house is way past due. As the birthdays started adding up, I took the plunge and bought a home. I was cautioned against it by a well-meaning friend, who suggested that I should wait to purchase a home because buying one said I had "settled in" and given up the notion of ever being married. This simply was not the case. I felt it was wisdom for me to purchase a piece of property. Married or not, to give away money (and that is what you are doing when you are renting) was not being a good steward of what God had blessed me with. The more practical outlook is that I now would have something to bring to my marriage whenever it comes to fruition. Real estate is one of the best investments you can make for a guaranteed increase in return. When my husband shows up, we will buy another house and have equity toward our future. Begin to think of ways you can add to your financial collateral on your own. It certainly sweetens your position as a newlywed. Every girl should have a dowry of sorts to share at will or simply to maximize her own security.

What about trips to exotic places? Why wait to have a romance in order to go? Perhaps romance is waiting for you there. Are you getting this? This is about making your life happen. When that man comes into your life, he should have to interrupt some things. The opposite of that situation is that you will completely overwhelm him by being too available and desperate for his attention to fill the gaps in your life. What a turnoff! Have you ever had a man who liked you waaaay more than you liked him? You couldn't get rid of him. He wanted all your time. What was your response? You were just not that into him, right? As a matter of fact, you ran from him as though he were the plague.

He was too needy, not intriguing enough, and perhaps even a little bit scary. Well, consider that in reverse. Are you grasping why your life has to happen first before you meet a man?

If you've read any of my other books, you know my favorite Scripture: "He who is full loathes honey, but to the hungry even what is bitter tastes sweet" (Proverbs 27:7). If you don't have a full and enriching life before you meet a potential mate, you will end up settling for someone you wouldn't ordinarily desire because desperation will make you accept anything. But a full life that is already satisfying at its core will make you much more discerning about your love choices simply because you can afford to take your time and get it right.

Having a life doesn't just answer the desperation question; it also sets the bar on the respect you will receive from a potential love interest. He will not take you or your time for granted because you had a life before you met him. You are now game waiting to be captured. A challenge. A prize. You need to make that man plot and plan how to get more of your time. Leave him wondering how to win you rather than hide from you. The fuller your life, the more fascinating you will be. The more stimulating conversation you will have to offer. The more he will love how he feels when he's around you and want to be around you more.

When you have a full life, there is no need for games or manipulation. Your life will take care of making you intriguing. The balance here is in the presentation of yourself to him. You should always be delighted to hear from him but not have enough time to run after him. Got it? Make him feel desired but not required—there is a difference. One makes you interesting. The other makes you a pest.

This, however, can be where many accomplished women lose their footing and come to the conclusion that they intimidate men and, therefore, there is no hope for them. Please know ahead of time that I base all of my comments on *men,* not boys. Again, there is a difference. A true man likes to have a woman on his arm who is about something. What he does *not* want is a woman who is overly impressed with herself. Leave some room for him to sing your praises. As a matter of fact, let him find out about you and all you have achieved little by little. Like pleasant surprises. There's no need to overwhelm. You want him to fall in love with *you,* the woman. Not your achievements or material acquisitions.

Be more interested in him than in yourself. Sometimes those who have accomplished a lot can be self-consumed, always in visionary mode. A man wants a woman who is present with him, interested in him, and impressed with what he brings to her life. He should be able to find ways to contribute to you feeling loved as well as contributing something tangible to your world. Leave room for that to happen. Which means in some cases, even if you can do something for yourself, let him do it. No man likes to feel unnecessary. He needs to make a space for himself in your world as well as in your heart. Find ways to celebrate him above what you have accomplished, and he will embrace your accomplishments with pride.

This is also the time to nurture rich friendships in two arenas. Other men and women. The state of your marriage will only be as rich as the friendships you take the time to cultivate. Here is where you learn everything that can be applied to your marriage. Open communication, sharing the important things. Working through offence. Expectations of giving and taking. Compromising. Being sensitive to the needs of others. Being a good listener. Nurturing a servant's heart. Being transparent and accountable to someone. Giving 100 percent of yourself unconditionally.

Yes, friendship is the rehearsal before the marriage. Platonic friendships with men are important because, let's face it, you cannot learn about men from your female friends. Men are different. They think differently. They rationalize on another wavelength. The way to learn about men is to observe men, talk to men, and listen to men. Most women gauge the responses of men based on their own responses to things. This is not the way to get an accurate read on a man. The assumptions we make when it comes to men usually send us careening down the path of self-deception, where we make destructive mistakes that not only affect the outcome of the relationship, but our hearts as well. Take the time to make and treasure your male friendships. Live, laugh, and learn from them. When men get honest, the revelations can be most surprising. They get honest when they feel safe, and they feel safest within the boundaries of a friendship that expects nothing more from them.

Now is also the time to spend time constructively nurturing your relationships with other women, as well as your family members. I am astounded by the number of people who desire to be married but have outstanding feuds with family members and inconsistent relationships across the board. It is self-deception to think that if you have unresolved issues with those you should be at peace with in your inner circle, you will be able to live through conflict with a spouse. All of your other relationships are tests for the graduate class called marriage. Settle your debts with those in your life now. Clean the slate and get your heart back to a healthy place, where it is free to give and receive love. Thinking that if you had the right mate all of your other relationship dramas would be resolved is not realistic. In contrast, getting married will exaggerate them. Trust me. Your marriage will bring all unresolved issues to light without fresh tools for resolving them.

The long and short of it? Never put off for tomorrow what you can do today. Never hang so much credence on someone else completing you that you leave the major issues of your life hanging in the balance. The question begs to be asked: If God told you that you would never be married, what would change about your approach to life? What would you get busy doing? How would your priorities shift? What would you do with the rest of your life? How would you apply yourself to the relationships that are already at hand? The truth of the matter is tomorrow is not promised. None of us can afford to allow life to pass us by on a maybe. This is also a good case for not abandoning your friends when the "man of your dreams" comes on the scene. Remember, your friends were there before he showed up, and they will still be there should he not last for the rest of love's journey.

When all is said and done, the only thing you can control is yourself and your outlook. You get to make your life as exciting as you want it to be. Don't leave that up to the discretion of another human being who could fail you. Not on purpose, but let's face it—life happens. So does death, disappointment, bad health, unemployment, and a plethora of unseen interruptions of our perfectly laid plans for happiness and fulfillment. Jesus said, "Do not worry about tomorrow, for tomorrow will worry about itself. Each day has enough trouble of its own" (Matthew 6:34). Even He, though having an omnipotent knowledge of things to come, practiced being present every day. Jesus completely submerged Himself in what lay before Him in the given moment. How much more should we, who do not have a full knowledge of what tomorrow holds, follow His example by being present—living in the fullness of where we are right now, right where we are?

 GETTING REAL

☙ In what areas have you been stuck in life?

☙ What will you begin to do differently?

☙ What would you do differently if you were not going to be married for the next five years?

☙ What things would you like to experience, trips would you like to take, and things would you like to see? What is stopping you?

So I commend the enjoyment of life, because nothing

is better for a [woman] under the sun than to eat

and drink and be glad. Then joy will accompany

[her] in [her] work all the days of the life God has

given [her] under the sun (Ecclesiastes 8:15).

KING SOLOMON,
after much thought at the end of his days.

Embracing the Cinderella Syndrome and waiting for the perfect prince to come rescue you

Just thinking out loud...

All his life he had dreamed of finding a love to call his own, and finally he had found her. She was the one he had searched for to have and to hold forever, amen. She made paying the price for her hand well worth it. She was so beautiful. So sweet. So desirable. He could hardly wait to claim her as his bride. She also found him to be all that she had longed for. Handsome and debonair. Sweeping her off her feet. One kiss reduced them to tears, so great was their passion for one another. Loving him was heaven on earth. They made plans for the future and counted the days until they would become one.

And then the blessed moment came and they were wed. What a celebration it was. Spirits as well as anticipation were high. At last the moment had come when they could pour their love out on one another without reservation. But the honeymoon night was a flurry, so caught up were they in the intoxication of the moment. And then it was over as quickly as it had begun. She was not the woman he had dreamed of. In her mind, neither was he. They retreated to separate corners, wondering what had gone wrong. Who had flipped the script on this love story? This was not the happy ending they had hoped for. Whose fault was it, and how would they weather the storm they now faced? All expectations aside, they both had hoped for something they did not receive. She, a husband who loved her unconditionally and celebrated her beauty, treating her as a precious find. He, a wife he desired more than anything, a partner and best friend he enjoyed sharing secrets with.

Instead, she got a husband who buried himself in his work and had an eye that wandered to someone he desired more than her. He found himself saddled with a woman he did not love, fathering children faster than he could foster his feelings for her. What had been a romantic dream turned into a nightmare for Jacob and Leah. (Their story is found in Genesis 29–35.) They suffered for it and so did their children, who were subjected to the awful truth that there was no love lost between their parents. How disappointing to leave this earth considering the love that could have been but never was and the years spent surviving instead of thriving with the person by your side.

And what about Rachel, the other woman in this love triangle? She was the one Jacob really loved, and due to the cruel manipulations of her own father, she saw the man she loved more than anything else being married off to her sister, Leah, instead. Even though Jacob worked another seven years for her father and married her also, Rachel's wonderful fantasy of how their years together would unfold were marred by the unpredictable circumstances she found herself in. Her union with Jacob was far from the perfect marriage she had envisioned.

I'm sure Leah also suffered. For a while there must have been the hope that the man who had been tricked into marrying her would come to love her in time. All it would take was her being the best wife she could be, blessing him with children to stoke his pride, and he would come around. But no matter how hard she tried, she was never embraced. Never celebrated. Never loved.

She was merely tolerated. She might have even felt used. Think of the lonely nights she spent knowing he was with someone he loved more. And even though Rachel was her sister, she was still the other woman, so the pain in Leah's heart didn't sting any less. Growing more disillusioned, feeling more rejected than ever, she probably transferred her love to her children, spoiling them in the hope of getting love from them that she never received from her husband. Not exactly the makings of a healthy, functional household.

It is safe to say we all have dreams or fantasies of our knight in shining armor showing up to carry us off on the white horse of our expectations. These dreams can become loftier and loftier as the years go by. Will he be handsome? Will he be rich? The longer we wait for our prince to arrive, the longer the list of our prerequisites grow. We can actually imagine ourselves right out of a good catch if we don't wake up from our slumber, smell the coffee, and take a sip of reality. When the fantasy becomes a bigger picture than the choices that stand before us, we are in trouble. Our insistence for exactly what we want can tie God's hands and cause us to accuse Him of failing to fill our requests.

Perhaps you've overlooked several possibilities that have been sent your way. Hmm…this is going to be a hot chapter, so let's get started.

LET'S TELL THE TRUTH AND SHAME THE DEVIL

    What are your top three requirements for the man of your dreams?

    How many of these attributes are lasting ones? How many of them affect your emotional and spiritual welfare?

    How important is chemistry to you?

    How does chemistry play into a lasting relationship?

Solution: Kill the fantasy

All right. It's time to roll up your sleeves and work with me on this one. I know it can get deep when you begin dealing with what you really want, but somebody has to break this down so we can get on with it. It's amazing to me how much energy we put into categorizing our "type" of man, and yet I find very few people ever marrying their type. This indicates to me that for the most part our "type" just "ain't right" for us most of the time. Now that statement just sent shivers up some sisters' spines, I know. I felt the earth move just from typing this. So let's consider this matter slowly. The cold hard facts, ma'am, are what we need to look at.

First of all, unless you are in college, where there is still plenty of room as well as activities geared for meeting new people who could be potential mates, your cache of options will be too limited for you to waste precious time insisting on things that won't affect the quality of your relationship one way or the other. That would include things such as these: He *has* to be taller than you or you won't consider him. He doesn't dress the way you would like him to. You want him to look like your favorite movie star or sports hero. He has to have lots of money. He has to sport a six pack and all of his hair. C'mon you know the list. Now shake it off and let's get down to business.

What is the benefit of having a pretty house if no one is at home? Or worse yet, someone is at home but there are no lights on upstairs, if you know what I mean. A handsome man is by no means a guarantee of a lasting relationship. It will take more than enjoying the view to keep the house standing and make the relationship work. Especially if you're fighting over the mirror.

The bigger question to ask yourself is what would you like your *relationship* to look like and then find someone who makes that happen. That person might come in a package you were not expecting. Now, don't get excited. Someone at a singles' conference I recently spoke at seemed agitated by the fact that most of her happily married friends had all registered the same comment in reference to their husbands. "I never thought I would end up with someone like him. He wasn't my type." This led her to ask me, "Why can't I have it all? If I want someone who is fine, what's wrong with that? Why would God make me fall in love with someone who looked like Quasimodo?" After I finished laughing I answered her. Please know that God is not a capricious Cupid running around shooting off arrows and making us fall in love with donkeys or men who look like Shrek, okay? He doesn't *make* us fall in love with anyone. The truth of the matter is that love responds to love, and sometimes you will be amazed to discover what love looks like!

The things a person does draws our heart to open and embrace them. How they make us feel about ourselves and them is totally up to what they say and do. This is what inspires emotions of love. What we must locate is not the person who looks like the man of our dreams, but the person who embodies the things we need in order to have a lasting and fulfilling relationship. When you look through the eyes of love, you will be amazed at what you are able to see. Love is a beautifier. So it's not a matter of if God will make you fall in love with an ugly person. The real truth of the matter is that love can make someone who is just easy on the eyes look amazingly gorgeous to you. So what is most important? That your eyes like what they see or that your heart feels happy and your relationship is secure? You decide.

Now someone is screaming, "But I must be attracted to him!" This is true. But I contend that most of us do not give people enough time to become attractive in our eyes. The most sustainable chemistry is one that builds slowly. Let's take a realistic look at chemistry. Chemistry is exactly that—a combustible situation that can blow up or be diffused in a moment's notice because there is nothing specific that one can point at to sustain it. Chemistry does not add up to long-term relationship, commitment does. As two people honor the commitment they've made to one another, love grows and respect deepens, causing desire and passion for one another to flourish.

Can I challenge you to a small experiment? The next time someone invites you out for coffee or dinner, say yes even if he is not your type. If you are honest with yourself, you don't know enough about him to know you don't like him, so consider this what they call in modeling a "go-see." You are going to see if you like him or not after you've given him an audience. Now, I'm going to stretch you. If you go out the first time and you decide you don't like him, unless you perceive that he is dangerous, go out with him again. Why, you ask? Because when people are nervous they do stupid things and everyone is nervous on the first date, so give it another shot. Who knows? Even if he doesn't turn out to be prince charming, at least he might be a good friend, and certainly as single women we should not turn down too many free dinners. Just kidding, but there's a smidgeon of truth to that. This is an exercise to merely stretch you beyond your norm and open you up to other possibilities. You might be pleasantly surprised.

Perhaps he's only 5'8" and matches you eye to eye, but he makes you laugh and loves your toe jam? Are you really going to tell me you're going to pass that up while you wait for Mr. 6'2" who is fine as wine but forgets your birthday and doesn't return your calls until three days later? Let's compare the feelings these two generate…hmm…it's not brain surgery to me.

Moving on, how about this one? He must be perfect. We don't really say that, but it is most certainly the implication. We want him to be chiseled and cut, the body beautiful. This can be a reasonable request if you have not crossed the 30-yard line, but beyond that, unless you go for a younger man, you might get a slightly different version of your wishes. This is a highly subjective thing; however, those who spend more time sculpting their body than polishing their character leave me lukewarm and unimpressed. You should feel the same way. Trust me, I'm all over that passage in Proverbs 31:30. You know: "Charm is deceptive and beauty is fleeting." In other words, it all goes south at some point in time, so something had better be left standing. The other part of this question is, are you what you desire? Someone who is into taking care of their body is highly conscious of that in other people. Mr. Buff Body is usually looking for *Ms.* Buff Body. We all tend to be a bit narcissistic, so be prepared to attract what you are.

Cast down all imaginations having to do with physical appearance. As one who formerly worked in the world of advertising, I know what it takes to make all those people you see on television and in print ads look good—a lot of time, greasepaint, and retouching. Take a look around you at the people in your world. That is what real life looks like. It is imperfect, but if you look closely, it is the flaws that make people interesting.

Perhaps the wonderful mate you search for will not be found in your race. Ooo, did all the air just get sucked out of the room? It amazes me how many people put restrictions on where love can come from. And yet isn't the bottom line that you want to be loved and give love? How much more will your options increase if you broaden your scope? Some would say they don't want to settle for less than what they want in a partner, but aren't you settling for being alone if you don't check out all the opportunities available for a fulfilling relationship? Are you open to being surprised by where you might find love?

Becoming a part of a global community that is quickly evolving with the times means becoming more open to the infinite possibilities of how God answers the cry of our hearts. He is well able to blend what we want with what He knows we need, but sometimes that comes in unexpected packages. The safer list to make would be attributes versus outward appearance. Rumor has it that though we judge by the packaging, God, who is much smarter than we are, is still far more impressed by what's in the heart. After far too many years of being moved by all the wrong things, I'm with Him.

It is crucial to your joy level to take note of one glaring truth—there are no perfect specimens of humanity. Everyone has a flaw, within or without. If he looks fabulous, guess what? At some point in time his breath stinks, he has gas, he passes wind. He has some little idiosyncrasy that is going to irritate you. And don't get it twisted. You have something that is going to get on his nerves too. I think God allows this on purpose so that we all learn to operate in grace. If we could look beneath the surface of the person to the things that are lasting and genuinely important, the opportunities for true love would increase in leaps and bounds.

Get past the way he dresses and all the other extraneous things that he may need you to fix. You are supposed to add to his life and make him a better man. He's been waiting for your touch to perfect him, to polish him. To take him to the next level of who God created him to be as a man. I remember talking to a friend who tells the story of how she was not attracted to her husband initially. I couldn't believe it because he is a truly happening, attractive brother. When I asked her why she hadn't been attracted to him, she said, "Honey, he didn't look like that until I got hold of him. You're looking at my handiwork!" So contrary to all the fairy tales, your knight may show up with some rusty armor that you'll need to polish. Your prince might need a different haircut. It's called customizing your man when you add your transforming signature to his wardrobe and even some of his habits, but then remember, ladies, he will be all yours. Though he may not be perfect by all obvious standards, he could be perfect for you if you take the time to discover all the potential beneath the surface. If you're up to the reality challenge, say "aye."

Moving on to doctors, lawyers, businessmen, and impresarios...every girl dreams of marrying one, but in the real world how many of these do you meet on a daily basis? Furthermore, have you ever spoken with the wives of these men? They are never at home! These ladies are, generally speaking, the loneliest women you will ever meet. Sorry to burst your bubble, but wealthy men are usually out making money until they feel they've made enough to pad their retirement funds or satiate their egos. If you measure a man's love by his presence, this might not be the love match you imagined.

But let's take a look at why most women dream of the handsome, rich prince coming to sweep her off her feet and carry her away. Don't we all wish we could be wooed by a handsome man despite our state of undoneness? But, again, this is where reality collides with fiction—waiting to be rescued usually leaves us... well, waiting to be rescued.

Is this line of thinking really fair? Let's turn the tables. You be the man for a minute. You've worked hard all your life to get where you are. To acquire what you've acquired. To get out of debt and secure security for your future. Then you meet this woman who doesn't have anything but a pretty face. She's sweet enough; bright too. Charming, witty...and she seems to really love you. But she has a pile of debt and doesn't seem to be intentionally taking the steps to be responsible for it. As a matter of fact, she's spending more money and wants you to subsidize some of her desires. How do you feel about that? Are you inspired to rescue her or grip your checkbook and credit cards and head for the hills? Life is hard enough. No one wants to acquire someone else's debt.

Of course, not all women looking to be rescued are focused on financial issues. Some want to be emotionally rescued. This too is a difficult position to put anyone in. First of all, they will never live up to your expectations. They will never be able to do enough to make you feel good about yourself. Therefore, the best way to free yourself is to settle these scores on your own. This will require discipline on your part, but ultimately it's worth the effort. The end result is that you will feel better about yourself and be more attractive to the prospects you encounter. There will be no baggage to hide and hope they don't find out about it until they are in too deep. No hard conversations to have that mar the glow of romance, and certainly nothing to foster resentment later in the relationship and leave room for your true intentions to be questioned.

Intentionally decide to be the "good thing" that a man finds instead of being a liability. If you are of the "I'm waiting to be rescued camp," you are entering the relationship with a huge strike against you that will cause problems later. The more you resolve your issues before entering a relationship, the freer you will be to enjoy it. Plus, honing your own survival skills prepares you to weather hard times whether married or single. In the course of life, your ability to overcome will be tested. Don't count on being rescued. You must be able to master life with or without the assistance of someone else because again—life happens. The thing or person you banked on for security could be gone tomorrow.

You've got to be able to sing "On Christ the solid Rock I stand, all other ground is sinking sand" and mean it. At the end of the day you have one consistent Provider. One amazing Affirmer. One who gives you validity. One who will love you in spite of yourself and never leave you or forsake you. In the meantime, in your personal fairy tale, perhaps the prince simply doesn't have enough rope to climb the tower you long to be rescued from or the knight has lost his horse as well as his way but he's limping toward you anyhow. Take a moment to look past the outfit to his heart and his intentions and be moved by the sheer strength of his character, his love, and his persistence. Don't allow the dragon to distract you from his pure intentions and the bright future he promises. Not exactly the package you expected? Oh, my sister, take another look. The contents are incredible.

GETTING REAL

◦ How has insisting on your type worked for you so far?

◦ Is your type a realistic standard?

◦ What do you want your relationship to look like? Will your type be able to make what you want a reality?

◦ What things or circumstances do you long to be rescued from? What will happen if no one rescues you?

◦ In what ways can you better secure these things for yourself? How will that make you feel?

When she saw her hope unfulfilled, her

expectation gone, she took another of her cubs

and made him a strong lion (Ezekiel 19:5).

THE PROPHET EZEKIEL,
talking about Israel's backup plan.

*Missing the significance
of the present moment*

Just thinking out loud...

There she was, toiling away. Doing what she had been doing for the last three months. Gleaning the leftovers dropped by those who harvested. One season had blended into another season, and nothing different had occurred in her life. Perhaps the sun had shifted. The air cooled somewhat from the first whiff of summer transitioning toward fall, but there were no new adventures. Still, she went about her work. There was actually a peace to it. Knowing what the day would bring. No surprises. She spent her hours composing her own personal songs under her breath. Feeling strength coursing through her limbs from subliminal exercise birthed out of simple hard work. She would not complain. After all, she had happened upon the field of one who had been gracious enough to provide her with meals and show her kindness.

She counted her blessings while finding new delights in the midst of where she presently stood. An unexpected flower found among the wheat. The color of it brightly contrasting against the sameness of its surroundings. The pleasant smiles of the other workers, who lifted their heads to extend a greeting, a joke, or a word of encouragement. These were things that added a layer of music to her internal symphony. Soon the season would be over and another would begin. The only certainty she had was in what was before her today; therefore, she would glean as much as she could and welcome the next day with fresh expectancy when it came. She would be present in this season and not try to anticipate what she could not embrace in the moment.

So lost was she in her present that she didn't notice when the wind shifted and his eyes lingered longingly on her. It was the advice of another that encouraged her to visit him on the threshing floor now that the harvest was complete. And then truly what had been planted came to bear sweet and lasting fruit above all that she had ever imagined. Um-hmm, while our girl Ruth just focused on pulling the fragments of her life together, she was noticed by a wealthy man named Boaz. The rest is history. (Read Ruth's story in the book of Ruth.)

It might be that life has dealt you a hand you don't particularly like—perhaps unexpected loss or you've simply waited for your heart's desire for far too long. How do you move forward when you don't know exactly where you're going or where the road may turn? Do you give in to feelings of resignation or bitterness? Or do you cope with what you have, seek to find the treasure among the rubble, and believe God for a brighter future? What does it take to get the life you want? Is it truly possible? Last I heard, with God all things are possible (Matthew 19:26)!

LET'S CONSIDER WHERE WE ARE RIGHT NOW

- What do you like about your life right now? What don't you like?

- What would you like to change?

- Is changing your circumstances within your power?

- What will you have to do in order to get the results you want?

- When will you begin taking the steps necessary to get what you want?

Solution: Embrace the season

Once in the middle of an extremely hot, humid summer, I spotted a woman walking down the street, bundled up from head to toe in a wool hat, scarf, long down coat completely zipped, heavy-duty boots, and mittens. You can imagine my dismay. I started sweating just looking at her. Others on the street were stepping around or avoiding her because obviously something was very wrong. She was not dressed for the season.

Perhaps some of us don't go as far as dressing in winter attire when it's summer or summer attire when it's winter, but internally we are completely oblivious to the seasons of our lives; therefore, we're always where we don't want to be and dreaming of the grass being greener on the other side. As I always say, the only reason it's greener is because someone is doing the work it takes to make it lush and beautiful. That being the case, if you did the same thing on your side of the fence, your grass could be just as green. Obviously, the one on the side with greener grass didn't spend a lot of time bemoaning the state of their lawn. They simply recognized the season for planting, the season for fertilizing, and the season for nurturing the seeds they had been given. They did the work it took to be able to harvest the results they wanted.

About now would be the time when you ought to stop asking why aren't you married and change the question. Change it to what are you supposed to be experiencing in your life right now? What things should you be cultivating? Where should your focus be? I firmly believe that when God doesn't get us out of a situation, it's because He wants to get something out of us. In my own life I believe He wanted me to do exactly what I'm doing right now. That is, writing and speaking to women all over the world on living, loving, and overcoming. This would never have happened if I had gotten married when I wanted to. It was out of my pain and dissatisfaction that I began to seek and find the answers I now share with you.

If I reflect on the pattern I fell into with all the men I had encountered in my life, I would have to admit I was more than a little chameleon-like, becoming whatever they needed or wanted. I became completely caught up in their world, their aspirations, and their dreams, much to the neglect of my own interests. God could not get what He wanted out of me. It took a season of me deciding not to pursue any type of relationship and focusing on exactly what I was supposed to be doing with my life to get myself on the path I am presently traveling. Now, can I have it all? A man and a writing and speaking career? Of course I can, but I understand it's not necessarily realistic to think that one can juggle everything at the same time. One area or the other would suffer from lack of focus. Something in my life would have to change. Priorities would have to shift drastically in order for me to be a good mate to the man God would give me. In time I will be willing to rearrange some things, but for now I'm happy and excited about life as it is, in full pursuit of my passions with no distractions to slow my progress. I am in my planting season. I also realize this season will pass.

But back to you. Have you been wondering what is wrong with you? I can tell you now that this is the wrong question. If you've been asking yourself the same thing over and over again and not getting an answer, it's time to ask yourself a different question. The right question would be, what season are you in? I always say the right person at the wrong time can be just as bad as the wrong person at any time. Maybe the partner God has for you is not ready, or perhaps *you* are not ready. God likes to give blessings that won't add sorrow to your life (Proverbs 10:22). Lots of things have to line up in order for a connection to be the right connection. Spirits and purposes have to be aligned so that they complement instead of compete against one another. It was with great thought and precision that God molded Eve to be a helper suitable for Adam. He has not stopped being a painstakingly careful matchmaker.

Ruth decided to focus on the immediate need before her—that of building a life for herself and her mother-in-law, while Orpah decided to go looking for another husband instead of continuing on with them. I assume this because when presented with the dismal forecast for husband shopping in Israel, she voted to return to Moab and we never hear from her again. I do hope she found what she was looking for, but we will never know. Orpah faded into obscurity with the rest of the women who make marriage their only goal in life. Now don't get excited. Being a wife is an honorable position, and a wife is a gift from God to her husband, but matrimony should not be what defines you as a human being. Though the Proverbs 31 woman was an amazing wife, she had a long list of contributions attributed to her at the end of the day. She had other interests and passions besides her husband and was noted for leaving a lasting impact not only in her home but also in her community. If your goal is only to be married, you will never blossom into all that God created you to be and the world will be seriously robbed of your touch and contributions.

Ruth wasn't looking for a husband, but she got one anyway, which is a clear indication to me that one doesn't have to spend their energy hunting for the perfect mate. Just be about the business of living and he will find you. The pressure that others put on you to validate your existence by nabbing a mate is just not how God operates. He is more interested in the seasons of your life, the process of your personal growth, and how you weather them. He understands that each season has a purpose, and He is all about seeing His purposes get fulfilled because they affect kingdom business at large.

It is essential that we not just recognize the season but also understand the *purpose* of each season. Can you imagine trying to plant in the wintertime? You would become awfully frustrated! The earth would be frozen. It would be difficult to dig up the ground to plant the seed. And even if you managed to plant the seed, it would probably never bear fruit because you wouldn't be able to water it. Water would freeze and destroy the seed. But if you planted it in early spring and nurtured it, you would see it begin to blossom as the heat and moist earth incubated it. Yes, there is a time for planting and seasons for growth, harvest, and rest.

Plant love and service to others. This is precious seed for your future. Grow in the knowledge of God and yourself. This is important. A lot of times people enter marriage not knowing who they really are or what they need. Somewhere along the way they decide their partner is not a good match for them. Grow and blossom as a woman. Grow in self-awareness of your giftings, of what you have to offer, of your strengths but also of your weaknesses. Own them and do the work to become greater than you already are. Then you will be at peace and able to harvest the right choices for your life. You can't reap what you have not planted. The unrest we sometimes experience comes not from just the fact that we are not experiencing harvest in our lives, but also from a subliminal fear that comes from the knowledge that we haven't planted anything toward our expectations.

The other thing you must consider is just because you want it to be a specific season doesn't make it so. It always tickles me when I get on the elevator in the summer and people are complaining about how hot it is. These are the same people who were complaining about the cold in the winter. I stand there saying, "I'm not going there. I'm going to appreciate the heat while we have it because it's not going to last." We're never satisfied! We are always so busy anticipating the next thing that we cannot enjoy the present. That is the root of an ungrateful spirit. What next? What next? What next? How could you even enjoy the next thing if you haven't taken note of where you are? What will you have to compare it to?

I found out a long time ago that complaining about where I was didn't make God move any faster to change things. It was only after I had released what I longed for and settled into where I was and what I already had before me that things would change. And not just settled in unwillingly. There had to be a major shift in my approach to where I was at the time. It was only after I embraced my present reality with joy and a grateful heart that things changed. What is the subtle lesson in this? I believe we are to learn to be content in all things so that our emotions cannot be manipulated by circumstances. Any situation that brings you joy could change tomorrow. Your ability to be consistently joyful and fulfilled must come from a source higher than what you possess or experience.

We, like Ruth, must learn to work with what we have and trust God to enlarge our lives based on what we are willing to be faithful with. After the death of her husband, she chose to follow Naomi to Bethlehem in Judah. They arrived at harvesttime. I think this is significant. She was scheduled to get something out of being willing to sow her life into the life of the one who immediately needed her. She could have been focused on what she did not have, or lingered in the place of mourning for her dead husband and all his death had cost her personally, but instead she decided that this season of her life was to be dedicated to Naomi. She worked through barley and wheat season before finally having the encounter with Boaz that changed the course of her life.

Now it was the end of the harvest season. The season that releases a man to commit to a woman. We have to be cognizant of the man's season as well as our own. He has to be in a season of readiness for a mate before he can commit to one. He has to be settled in his heart about the level of fruitfulness in his life. If he feels he cannot take care of a woman, it will keep him from committing even if he wants to because his fear of rejection will overrule his desire for the woman he wants. Therefore, when a man tells you he is not ready for a commitment, you should believe him. He knows instinctively when he is ready. He is not only wired spiritually to know when it is time, he also has an intellectual clock that releases him to seek commitment when his affairs are in order. A man is unable to rest in a relationship until his ability to provide for his woman has been settled. He must be on solid footing and see his way clear in order to be able to rise up to his full stature as a man. Otherwise, he simply does not feel comfortable asking her to take a significant role in his life. Be sensitive to this and allow him the room he needs to get his life in order. You should honor him for wanting to be the right kind of partner to you. My only caution in this is not to allow him to drag this out interminably. This could be a sign of other issues in his character, such as self-involvement or commitment phobia. Don't make life so comfortable for him that he does not feel the need to commit (but we'll cover that in a later chapter).

In the meantime, you should be busy gleaning from your present life knowledge, experience, and wisdom. You should be sowing seeds in the lives of those around you in significant ways. Giving and serving now gets you in the habit of giving and serving in your marriage. You will be well acquainted with the joy that can be yours when you apply yourself to the awesome privilege of imparting something from yourself into the lives of others. Know that what you plant will be what you harvest. Plant good seed into the life of a man by being a sister. I've often joked about the fact that I've prepared many a man for another woman. I believe when I receive my husband that someone will have sown into his life to groom him into an extraordinary mate for me.

Get busy in your church and your community. Go the extra mile at work. You never know who is watching and checking out your heart, as well as noticing how you respond to life and all that it throws at you. Take advantage of the time you have at your disposal to prepare a rich harvest for yourself.

Now, just because you've planted seed doesn't mean that the harvest will be immediate. One has to wait for the seed to come to maturity. So know there will be a period of waiting. And just because you don't see anything blossoming right away doesn't mean that nothing is happening beneath the surface. There is a whole lot going on before a flower breaks through the soil. A seed is dying. The husk of that seed is falling away, releasing its contents into the earth. Then growth begins. Roots stretch to dig their way deeply into the soil to anchor themselves and solidify their placement in order to support the plant that will be reaching upward.

There is a lot going on inside of you preparing you, as well as your mate, to give and receive the love you want. To have a successful, committed relationship. That is, if you are willing to do the work, plant the seeds, and give God the time He needs to finish the work He has begun in you and in your partner. When He has perfected that work, the fruit of it will be ready for picking and everyone around you will be able to partake of the rich fare that comes out of your union.

Is there anything wrong with you? Probably not. People get married every day who have a ton of unhealthy baggage and things wrong with them, so this cannot be the criteria. If you are open to the Lord's leading and accountable to His Word, if you are one who is open to correction and personal growth, it's time for you to consider the fact that your singleness may just be a matter of God's timing for your life in light of His purpose and overall design for you. Chock it up to the season you are in. Sometimes seasons seem to last longer than we think they need to, but God is the master vinedresser. He knows best the time it takes to produce sweet fruit and a rich, rewarding harvest. This much we do know—the seasons eventually change, and usually by the time they do we conclude it was worth the wait.

GETTING REAL

What season are you in?

What would you like your harvest to look like?

What seeds are you planting toward that end?

What things are you presently gleaning in your life?

How is your time of planting affecting others in your life?

For everything there is a season, and a time for every

matter under heaven (Ecclesiastes 3:1 NKJV).

KING SOLOMON,
after considering all the events of his life.

Being shortsighted about life

Just thinking out loud...

They were on their way to a wedding...little did they know how late the groom was going to be. They were pressed and dressed to impress. Hair freshly coiffed. Nails newly done. Smelling fresh as daisies, they started their trek toward the venue. But the journey took them longer than anticipated. Finally reaching the agreed-upon site where they were to meet the groom before continuing, they waited and waited and waited. It grew dark. Weary from waiting, they fell asleep.

As they slept, their lamps grew dim. Some flickered out, leaving only the yawning darkness to surround them. Suddenly, the sounds of celebration could be heard in the distance. They awoke with a start, elated the bridegroom had finally come. Hastily they refreshed themselves and prepared to meet him and those who accompanied him. This was when the oversight was noticed. Half of them who were foolish did not have enough oil in their lamps to continue the journey. Turning to the other half of the wedding party, they asked if they could have some of theirs. But they, not relishing the thought of running low on provisions when the length of the journey was still unsure, suggested they go in search of their own oil, lest they also run out. So off went the wise ones with the bridegroom into the wedding feast, while the foolish ones went in search of more oil. By the time they got back the door had been bolted, their names were no longer on the guest list, and they were left on the outside looking in. (Read the parable of the ten virgins found in Matthew 25:1-13.)

Far too many women have uttered these words: "I thought I would be married by now!" The best-laid plans of mice and men can sometime go awry. Again, if you knew that you were never going to get married, what would you do differently with your life? If you knew your knight in shining armor wouldn't show up until five years from now, what would you do in the time afforded to you? You must take into consideration that tomorrow is not promised, and even if the day comes, the events of the day are subject to yield their own surprises. You never know—therefore, be prepared for what tomorrow could bring.

LET'S TAKE INVENTORY

- How have you prepared for your future with or without a mate?

- How would your future security be affected if you never got married?

- What things have you acquired that will contribute to your well-being in the future?

- What type of things do you need in order to feel more secure?

- In what ways do you need to be provided for? What resources do you have to address this need?

Solution:
Get a vision for your future

What do you want your life to look like? Go for it! Now is the time to put the wheels in motion, no holds barred. Many single women do not plan for their future because they are subliminally holding on to the dream that some man with a solid bank account will come along to rescue them at the last minute and make up for all the time they didn't save money, make sound investments, or do any of the groundwork for those years when they won't be spry, cute, and able anymore.

Somewhere in the back of their minds ('cause I know I'm not talking about you), they put off saving the way they should. After all, a man was supposed to show up and bring security for the future with him. What about embracing the thought that nothing is guaranteed? How many horror stories have you heard or read where a woman's husband has had an unfortunate end and she was left with nothing, not even enough to bury him? If tiny ants know they need to sock away supplies for a rainy day, how much more should we get a clue that now is the time to be realistic about the future?

The popular rule of finance is that one should have savings that amount to six months of your monthly budget should anything happen to you that affects your ability to work and generate income. But what about beyond six months to retirement? To the rest of your life? We are being warned daily that the future of Social Security is shaky at best and most people's lifestyles extend beyond what their present paycheck or a pension will support. Of course, we factor in trusting God to supply for us, but faith without works is dead, my sister. We must be wise and plan for the future. And in order to plan for it, we must envision it first.

I find myself caught between two cultures. The African side of me sees a culture that lives mostly on a cash basis. It is understood that if you want to acquire land, houses, cars, etc. that you must save for it and then purchase it when you have the money. Sometimes it takes people years to complete their house because they complete it as they get the money for it. But when they move in that house is paid for!

In America we can get in trouble easily because there is so much credit available. We are almost encouraged to be in debt. It's easy to believe you can have everything you want because you can pay for it later. The scary part is when the things to be paid for accumulate into a mountain that overwhelms your banking account and you find yourself living anxiously from moment to moment. I've been a victim of this along with countless others before learning that restraint is best for peace of mind.

King Solomon in his latter days said money answers everything (Ecclesiastes 10:19). I can see where he was coming from, as most people's woes seem to center around financial worries. I'm not trying to scare you, but we must soberly consider our future if we are to be wise women. If prince charming arrives late or not at all, we need to be prepared to live out our tomorrows free from the angst of severe lack. What are some of the ways we can get on track? Well, the rule of thumb is your first ten percent goes to God, the second ten percent should be put into savings, and then you can live off of the remaining balance.

In a perfect world another tenth should go into investments. If that's stretching it for you, then you need to consider a realistic amount but put something away regularly. When you get in the habit of saving, it becomes second nature to you and you'll be amazed at how money adds up over time, no matter how insignificant what you put aside seems to be. So, lady, make sure you have some savings. I always recommend a savings account you can dip into for emergencies and one at another bank you can't get to easily that you never touch.

Make an appointment with a financial counselor and begin a portfolio. You can decide if you want to go high risk or take conservative chances. This is another thing that grows with time. The key is to diversify. Never bank everything on one thing. Purchase a piece of real estate. In a perfect world it would be good to have some income property and a place of your own, but at least have one of these options. Even Oprah says land is the best investment 'cause God isn't making any more. This is an investment that is pretty much a guaranteed profit at a greater rate of growth than a bank account that collects only so much interest.

Is all this talk of money giving you a headache? It's okay—this too shall pass. The bottom line is you should deal realistically with the fact that just because you get a husband doesn't mean he will be the ultimate provider. Again, life happens. And one should not get married merely to procure financial security. It's not just money that you should focus on when looking toward the future.

Let's talk about equipping yourself for the journey. Being aware of all the things it takes to live a balanced life. A girl has got to acquire skills for the long haul. You don't have to become an expert, but you must have some savvy about the business of life. There are so many elements involved in functioning from day to day. Becoming resourceful in order to stay on top of life is a major coup. I'm talking about the mechanics of taking care of your car to simple handyman things around your house. I mean, beyond filling the tank with gas, would you know when something was wrong with your car? Do you know how to change the oil? Do you have a network of people in your life who can give attention to the things you can't handle?

On the one hand, a man needs to feel needed. On the other hand, what if he doesn't show up? A girl needs to know how to do some things for herself. So here's my suggestion: You should have a basic working knowledge of the things that might challenge you or affect your daily operations, backed up by people who really know what they are doing and who can take the ball and run with it if need be. When your man comes into your life, you are then released from having to cover all the bases. As I always say, a woman should never do what a man can do if one is around. In the meantime, sistahs are doing it for themselves.

It's not a good idea to make your primary goal that of being a homemaker. Get some life skills and some career skills while you are at it. Too many women end up eyebrows to scalp after they find that their husbands have left them in one way or another. Many women remain in abusive situations because they are not equipped to leave. They poured themselves into being a wife and never developed marketable know-how that can be applied to a job to take care of themselves and their children. There is a sense of powerlessness that can overwhelm a woman when homemaking is all she knows.

Whether you are in a happy marriage or not, it can be a healthier place for a husband and a wife when both of you bring skills to the relationship that empower working toward a richer life together. Should you choose to put your career on the back burner in favor of being a stay-at-home mom or an amazing housewife, that is fine. At least you know you've got an arsenal in your back pocket should you ever need it or decide to broaden your scope in later years.

Consider your additional skills a gift to your husband as well. In these times of financial stress, the burden on a man to carry the full load can push many over the edge. Knowing that his woman has skills that can contribute to their mutual dreams is a welcome relief to him. This brings an element of peace to the household as you plan and birth your future together.

Keep in mind the fabulous résumé that is so celebrated in Proverbs 31. Not only was this woman a homemaker, she was the consummate mother, wife, employer, entrepreneur, real estate maven, charitable philanthropist, counselor...whew! She had it going on. The woman had skills, yet she also had the wisdom to balance all these things according to the seasons. She did not rob her family of quality time, but as their lives transitioned so did hers. This was why she was able to laugh at the days to come and not be concerned about winter. She was prepared. She had given careful thought to her tomorrows and all those beneath her charge and plotted her course. She didn't wait until the last minute and then get overwhelmed with preparation. She did a little at a time, accumulating what was needed to face the days ahead comfortably.

This should challenge your spirit, my sister. Live redeeming the time while preparing for your future. In this world of immediate gratification, few think about tomorrow because they are far too entrenched in the now. Remember that right now will be the past shortly and tomorrow awaits you whether you are ready or not. Plan for your tomorrows but keep your balance by embracing your present.

Next on the agenda is you. The things we do to ourselves without thinking about what it will cost us in the future. This includes how you take care of your body. Many a woman has wept as past decisions now affect her ability to have children or cause worse health problems now that she is in a happy marriage. Everything from weight gain to anorexia, diet pills to abortions, surgeries to tattoos that have had bad effects on the body you now want to present to the man you love. "If I knew then what I know now" or "If only I hadn't done that. I never thought of what it would cost me." Many of the things we regret are things that could have been avoided if a little more time had been taken to ponder the course of our actions or simply get enough information to make an informed decision. Our life is an accumulation of choices we will be forced to own. Unfortunately, the payment on some of those choices is due at the most inconvenient times.

In the area of our hearts I find this to be most true. After subjecting yourself to far too many relationships that end badly, there's nothing left by the time a really good and deserving man comes along. Perhaps this is one of the reasons why God cautions us to guard our hearts (Proverbs 4:23). We can subject them to so much unnecessary heartache that it becomes impossible to celebrate love when it is finally safe to do so. It's interesting that we never consider the future when dealing with our hearts. If we are honest, there have been some men we have met in life that we knew were not the answer and yet we ignored the red flags and jumped into the pool with both feet. We will talk more about being heart-smart later, but suffice it to say that our choices today have everything to do with our internal health and our capacity to give and receive love in the future.

Nothing is really temporary. The things we consider fillers sometimes take on greater dimensions on the canvas of our lives than we ever dream. We've watched enough movies to know how the one little thing that was overlooked by everyone involved at the time turned into something that affected everyone in ways that could not be measured. "I never thought it would be that deep." "It was just a joke. Just one night. Just a fling. Just a thing to do…" But now it's suddenly so much more with lasting repercussions. Nuff said.

Close your eyes and dream of the perfect life. Every aspect of it. Your emotions. Your body. Your relationships. Your home. Your job. Your finances. Your children. Your pets. Your social life. See them clearly. In order to have what you see, you have some decisions to make about what you are going to do and what you are not going to do. About what you are willing to sacrifice. What you will not settle for. Like an athlete you have to master your emotions, your body, and your habits. You must exercise discipline. For example, you've got to get into that dress for your class reunion and you do what you have to do to lose ten pounds in two weeks. I'm talking about that kind of fierceness in your focus and your decision making. "Uh-uh, girl. I've got ten pounds to lose by next Monday. You'd better get that cheesecake out of my face…it sure looks good, though." That's what I'm talking about. I'm talking about owning your life from start to finish. Waiting for the main course and turning down all appetizers. Remember, you don't need a bunch of men and horrible experiences. You only need the one man God knows is best for you. You don't need cheap thrills and moments of immediate gratification that will cost you a lifetime of sorrow. The desire to scratch where it itches right now often gets us in trouble. It gets us off track and makes us miss our turn on the way to where we really want to go. I refuse to go out like that. How about you?

Close your eyes and retrieve that mental picture of the life you know can be yours to have. Hold on to it and make the choices that will lead you there.

GETTING REAL

ᏣᏁ What decisions have you made in the past that you regret now?

ᏣᏁ How have those choices affected your present?

ᏣᏁ How can they affect your future?

ᏣᏁ In what ways can you get back on track and redirect your path?

ᏣᏁ What heart decisions do you need to make going forward toward the life you want?

Make level paths for your feet and take only

ways that are firm (Proverbs 4:26).

Very good advice from a father that
any daughter could use.

Falling down on the job of life

Just thinking out loud...

It was standing tall and strong, its branches spreading out in every direction and filling the air. By all appearances, this tree was healthy and fruitful. Its lush leaves were rich, green, and inviting. A group of men approached. One of them drew near and searched among its leaves for fruit. Finding none, he uttered something quietly and then departed. The tree, not comprehending his disappointment, continued standing, watching until they disappeared into the distance.

And then it started. Deep beneath the surface, life began to escape its roots. Creeping upward, dryness set in, disfiguring its trunk, withering its leaves, and bowing its frame. It died slowly by degrees, day-by-day, until no sign of life remained. And then they returned—the same men who had passed before. One stopped short, staring in dismay. "Look, Master. The tree you cursed has died!" It felt so undone beneath his gaze. His eyes, though filled with compassion, offered no comfort. They moved on, and the tree mourned for days gone by when it was upright and strong, bearing fruit in its season. Now barren, cold, and dry, it had nothing left but memories of days when it had a rich bounty to give to others.

Jesus was hungry that day when He first spotted the fig tree.

In search of fruit, He looked between the leaves for something that would give Him sustenance. Surely this tree had something to offer; it certainly gave the appearance of fruitfulness. Disappointingly, it promised more than it was able to give. And so He went His way, decreeing it would never have the opportunity to disappoint anyone else who might be deceived by its appearance. (Read the story of the unfruitful fig tree in Mark 11:12-22.)

Many have perfected the art of walking through life with the appearance of boundless potential yet living unfruitful lives. They wonder why the days stretch on interminably, each the same as the one before, uneventful. "What is the meaning of life?" they ask. "Is this all there is?" Some feel as if they are a piece of merchandise that has been inspected and rejected repeatedly. They long for the day when that one man will find them to his liking and take them home. What is the magic formula, the missing ingredient for creating a life of fulfillment and love? The answer is found in what you give, not what you receive.

LET'S GET BENEATH THE SURFACE

ᥫ What do you have to offer to the mate God sends to you?

ᥫ What things of significance will you add to his life?

ᥫ What are you presently giving to others in your world?

ᥫ In what ways are you being fruitful?

ᥫ How can you be a greater source of blessing to those around you?

Solution: Rise to the occasion

Productivity. Now there's a word you can either love or despise. Productivity is the goal of any successful business. Hours of endless analysis are spent trying to discover what can increase the output of their employees and increase revenue. The value of any business is measured by its ability to generate a service or a product in order to increase the profit of the overall company and its employer. That profit margin is the measuring stick of success or the indicator of failure, should there be no profit. Based on this bottom line, it is determined if the business is a valuable entity or a liability.

Businesses are not the only things that get assessed. People do too. The value of a person is not assessed by what he or she receives, but rather by what he or she gives. The contributions they make to society. To their communities, their places of employment, their churches, their homes. Singles have long battled with the stigma of being second-class citizens. Not taken seriously, singles are sometimes viewed as a group of people who have nothing to contribute because of their pursuit of the perfect mate.

The apostle Paul, a single man responsible for writing much of the New Testament, gave his opinion on the single life by stating that he preferred for everyone to be single (1 Corinthians 7:7). He felt this empowered men and women to give themselves in service without the distraction of caring for a spouse (1 Corinthians 7:34). Yet many singles do not share this viewpoint. They don't view their time of singleness as a time of taking advantage of the rare freedom they possess to serve others and fulfill their life purpose with passion. In the end, many are as bad as the unfruitful fig tree. Looking good and all adorned in the latest fashion but leading unproductive lives. The fact should not be overlooked in the search for a mate that everyone is looking for the same thing. Someone to add something to their lives. To enrich them. To improve the quality of the life they already possess. How does one do this? By rising to the occasion. Looking past the immediate desires we possess to finding the richness in fulfilling our purpose and living as men and women who have a determined destiny.

I think of Jesus and the time He spent on earth. He was not distracted. He knew exactly why He was here. He was on a mission. He was not one to wander off course into areas that were not conducive to leading Him closer to His destiny. He was not caught up in His personal desires. He had died to them, aligning Himself and walking in tune with the heartbeat of His Father. Determined to fulfill His calling, He would not be deterred by temptation, the demands of others, or even the distractions of His inner circle. He would not be swayed by the tyranny of the urgent. He refused to be moved off His mark. He was after a bride, and in the end He sacrificed everything in order to have her. The route He took did not look as if it would lead Him to the place of ultimately getting His desire, but it did. He rose to the occasion, redeeming a world from sin and shame and in the end will get to claim the prize He so deeply desired—a spotless bride (the church) that was birthed out of His earthly mission.

We too have been fashioned with great purpose in the mind of God. He created us and named us after His divine purposes. In the midst of fulfilling the purpose for which we were created, we glorify God and reach the pinnacle of fulfillment we all so desperately crave. Small wonder the battle for our attention rages. If the enemy of our souls could keep us distracted by our own needs, we could spend a lifetime spinning our wheels and never get anything done! We could spend all our time working on our figures, our wardrobes, our careers, or finding the perfect mate and be asleep on our real job—that of fulfilling our purpose. Of touching and affecting the lives of others by what we impart to them on a daily basis by example, word, or deed.

If our only conversation is the state of, the lack of, or pursuit of a romantic relationship, we do everyone around us a disservice. We have so much more to offer. It's time to rise to the occasion and show the world that singles are a force to be reckoned with. We are intelligent, resourceful, and major contributors to the world at large. It's time to get busy being fruitful, productive, and a blessing to the lives of those around us. Our presence should offer sustenance to those in need.

One of the reasons so many spend so much energy searching for someone to complete them is because they don't fully believe that completion comes from a life lived purposely. The longing for affirmation is really from the deep-seated desire that has been placed in your spirit to do something that matters. Something that will be noticed as being valuable. Validation that your life is worth living after all. That *you* matter. That what you do has a lasting effect beyond your personal sphere. In the greater scope of life, to matter to the world surpasses one person stamping you with a mark of approval. Small wonder those who make tremendous strides in the area of contribution to the masses seemingly walk alone. Marriage is not the uppermost thought on their minds. These are people driven by a passion greater than that of romance. Their hearts have been caught on fire for fulfilling their purpose, fueled by the determination to leave the world a better place than they found it.

Someone is yelling, "Yeah, Michelle, but all the major contributors of the world were not single. Some of them were married." This is true, but I could also come back and say that if you did a poll, you would find that their spouses sacrificed a lot by having mates who were driven by their goals. They spent time alone while their spouse dedicated themselves primarily to their inner call, thus justifying Paul's statement about being single versus married. When you are married, your first priority of service must be to your spouse and family. When you are single, you are free to pursue your passions to the utmost, unhindered by familial distractions.

The fact that Rick Warren's *The Purpose-Driven Life* took the world by storm confirms that there is something more in demand these days than romance. Everyone wants to know why on earth they are here! We are here simply to be who we are to the glory of God. What does that mean? Each of us has been given the gift of significance inherent in our very nature simply by how we have been designed and wired by the hand of God.

Each of us will have a profound effect on someone in a moment when we are most unaware. Something we say or something we do will literally change the course of someone's life. We might never know the moment or the day it happens, yet we are all so interconnected that it is impossible not to touch someone on this journey through life. Here is the deep part. We literally get to choose how many times we touch others by purposing to intentionally do so! We have the power of choice. We get to partner with God, seek His face, and get direction on how we can be most effective and fruitful in our personal world as well as in the world at large.

This can sound like an overwhelming goal if you don't grasp the simplicity of what walking intentionally looks like. This is where you need to locate yourself and your personal gifts in order to know how this can play out in your own life. Recently I was speaking to a lady who had attended my first Diva conference. She said to me, "I don't know what my gifts are." So I asked her, "What is the thing everyone celebrates about you that you think is no big deal?" She shrugged and said, "Well, everyone thinks I'm very organized." This led to a discussion about how organized she was and how she loves for everything to be in its place. I then went on to tell her that everyone is not organized. This was a foreign thought to her. I pointed out to her that this is why her skill of organization was a gift. I went on to tell her of a woman who had established a business and made millions off of organizing people. She went into people's homes and businesses and made sense out of their chaos. She was absolutely amazed! It was then that I drove the concept home to her that our unique gifts have the capacity not only to bless others, but also to profit us in ways we can't imagine.

Paul, my favorite apostle, wrote to one of the churches and informed them that his life was all about taking hold of that for which Christ took hold of him (Philippians 13:12). In other words, God saw something in him worth coming after. Paul was dedicating his life to the pursuit of rendering that thing worthy of all of Christ's hard work on his behalf. You also have a "that." What are the things that resound with you? What things do you naturally enjoy? What things get you upset? These are all clues to your purpose. How many times have you said, "Somebody ought to do something about that!" Perhaps that someone is you. As a matter of fact, I know it is because you are the one who has been moved by that issue. Who best to address that problem? Who best to be a blessing to someone in need?

The only difference between those who excel in life and those who lead a mediocre existence is that one decided to do something about what they saw and the other one decided to wait for someone else to do it. Daily your prayer should be, "Lord, help me to touch and enrich someone's life today. Give me an opportunity to serve someone in need." Now, that is a prayer God is happy to answer. Perhaps the fear of what He might require of you is too great and stops you from declaring your availability to be used by Him. I say, go for it. Walk on the wild side. Dare to live dangerously. This is when life gets exciting.

It is in the impromptu moments of life that true fulfillment and joy are found. In the moment when you speak words of encouragement and cheer to someone who is downcast. When you listen to someone who just needs to talk. When you validate someone else's efforts. When you do your best at work as unto God in spite of a difficult boss. When you embrace the day, even though you have no physical arms to hold you. When you expand the world you live in by looking beyond yourself to the needs of others and actually do something about making a difference, you begin to experience a value-added life. You become a force to be reckoned with. You move past the place of taking up space to becoming a contributor to the world. Fruitful and productive.

Consider yourself a tree. What would you like others to find on your branches? Can you imagine the joy of having them find fruit that is tasty and gives them sustenance? That fills and nourishes them? That makes them stronger? Don't allow them to walk away disappointed and hungry because you had nothing to offer. There is no time like the present for living your best life. If things are not what you like or desire, dig deeper. Dig deeper into God. Ask questions. Seek direction on where your focus should be right now and then follow His direction. Dig deeper into your own heart, locate your passions, and follow them. They will reveal your purpose. Dig deeper into the lives of those around you. Be more aware of the needs of your friends, family, coworkers, and even strangers when you cross their path. It is in the reaching out to love unconditionally that love becomes attracted to us. Practice being present, living in the here and now, looking for opportunities to be a blessing right where you are today. Be proactive. Don't wait for life to push you this way and that. Chart your course and make things happen. Answer the call of God. Embrace what you were created to do and go for it. Nothing could be more liberating or satisfying than to know at the end of the day that you did something that made a difference to someone. Perhaps it was just a smile. A touch. You may never know how something you did brought someone back from going over the edge. It might be something more of note.

All I'm saying is at the end of the day there is no such thing as a meaningless contribution if it came from the center of your spirit. It was enough in that moment to promote change and set God's purposes in motion. For this reason you were created to fulfill your destiny in divine moment after divine moment for as long as you shall live, single or otherwise. Remember, when your life is summed up, it will be your contributions that will be noted, not your marital status.

GETTING REAL

~ What type of fruit do you have on your tree?

~ What would you like to have more of?

~ What types of needs do you see around you that you could address?

~ What would give you a tremendous sense of accomplishment?

~ If a reporter interviewed those who knew you, what would you want them to say about you? What do you need to do to earn that sort of review?

I press on to take hold of that for which

Christ Jesus took hold of me (Philippians 3:12).

PAUL,
contemplating his purpose on earth.

MISTAKE
NUMBER SEVEN

Being completely self-involved

Just thinking out loud...

He had a calling on his life. He was to begin the deliverance of his people. He was gifted. Sharp. Seemingly invincible and on top of his game, his pathway to success was diverted by his pre-occupation with himself. Enjoying one indulgence after another, the call on his life became a fuzzy memory lost beneath layers of feasting, partying, and falling in love with the wrong women. Women who appeased his flesh but added nothing to his spirit. The deeper his self-indulgence, the less his accountability to those who worried about his welfare. The less accountable he grew, the more proud and obstinate he became. Ignoring the danger signs, his character along with his discernment dissipated, leaving him obsessed with nothing conducive to fulfilling his calling.

Delving deeper and deeper into the entrapment of his own flesh, he forsook good decisions and clung only to those contributing to his immediate need for self-gratification. Believing his own press might have been his worse mistake. A mistake he discovered far too late. Deeply entwined in the arms of one with bad intentions, his lusts turned him over to those who blinded him and placed him in a bondage he never anticipated. In the throes of regret, he realized that pleasing himself had cost him everything.

In his last days Samson was able to come to himself, but it was too late to be redeemed physically from his mistakes. In one last valiant effort to live up to his calling, he sacrificed his life. It was a large price to pay for a few passing moments of guilty pleasures. (Read Samson's story in Judges 13–16.)

It's easy to rationalize that you owe it to yourself to fluff up your flesh every now and then when you feel you've been denied. The longer you feel confined in your singleness, the more your flesh cries out for rewards to silence it back into submission. But one indulgence usually leads to another and another...until you find yourself held captive by needs that overwhelm your will-power. What are you to do when you want what you want? Here is where that awful s-word comes in. It's called self-discipline, a thing that must be mastered if one is to have any kind of life at all.

LET'S COME CLEAN ON THIS ONE

ℭ What temptations are presently distracting you from your course in life?

ℭ How do you console yourself when reflecting on your single status?

ℭ In what ways does this self-indulgence make things worse?

ℭ What is the trap the enemy sets for you when you are feeling vulnerable and alone?

ℭ How can indulging in this further complicate your life? How can it rob you of your blessing?

Solution: Get over yourself

Everything surrounding us promotes our self-indulgence. *You deserve it. You owe it to yourself. Why not? You only go around once!* But actually those are lies. We go around more than once, and the second time is eternal. What we do will last and speak volumes to us about the choices we made. It is those moments of weakness that cost us the most. It all comes down to one flaw that pervades our humanity, that of selfishness. Our inability to hold our flesh and its desires at bay and fight its demands.

However, this is not just a fleshly thing. It can be mental. It can be an attitude. A feeling of entitlement. Of being owed pleasure in exchange for enduring the life one feels they have been compelled to live, and not of their own volition. A mindset that one is *owed* pleasure in some other form if one cannot be married. This is a dangerous trap for singles. This is the breeding ground for a host of bad habits that in due course culminate in severe losses or one being set in their ways and good for no one other than themselves. It's a catch-22. The more self-indulgent we become, the more we will find missing or wrong in our lives. It's like standing in front of a mirror and staring at your reflection incessantly. You will find a pimple if you look long enough. Or as my mother used to say, if you look for trouble you will find it. Well, getting stuck on self is truly looking for trouble. Self-awareness usually leads to some sort of self-indulgence to fill the gap left from examining one's belly button too long and coming to the conclusion that the void must be filled with some*thing* if not some*one*.

"If I can't have the one thing I want, then certainly I should be able to have everything else I want" is a pervasive attitude among singles. This type of self-indulgence and selfishness is downright unattractive. Life is not about any one person but how we all connect and affect one another as a whole. Therefore, life can never be just about you. And yet it is, isn't it? Your time. Your personal space. Your money. Your heart. When it comes down to it, this leaves us wide open. Vulnerable to offence because everything is taken personally when the focus is on you and you alone. But let's take these one at a time.

Your time. Is it really your time? Or do you see the time you have as a gift? A gift to be shared with others. Appreciated in moments alone but above all things giving of yourself even when it is not convenient. This is a most incredible act of grace. It's something that makes others feel valuable. That you took the time to give of yourself, with no bells, whistles, or hidden terms or clauses attached not only blesses the other person, it enriches you as a person as well. When you spend time with others simply listening, you accumulate a wealth of knowledge that can only bring depth to you as a person. To understand the heart of another, to increase in the understanding of human nature, makes you a richer person, who in the giving finds the getting to be more than what was parted with in the exchange.

Isolation forms a box around a person's spirit. An invisible prison where the imagination has room to overwhelm you with deception and fears that should not be acknowledged because they are of no consequence. I'm not talking about quality time spent with God, meditating on His Word, or the quiet time you spend in rest, renewing your body and getting your spirit aligned to face life. I'm speaking of selfish time. Where you lose yourself in you to the point that everything else becomes an intrusion. When the needs of others are ignored or, even worse, diminished to trivia first in your eyes and later in your comments and actions. In the end those who overindulge in isolation actually repel the love they want and find themselves very lonely people. Selfishness is prophetic in the sense that it promotes self-defeating behavior.

But what about personal space? Well, how personal is it? Having someone in our life would be the end of our personal space as we now know and treasure it and yet we insist on it. We guard the violation of our privacy with a fierceness that would rival a Doberman pinscher. Don't you *dare* just drop by without calling first! Okay, again here I am caught between cultures. The hardest adjustment for me when I first began visiting my father in Ghana was what I termed the audacity of people to just stop by any time of day or night without calling before they came. They would patiently wait until you got your clothes on and came down from your room to greet them. I was highly annoyed until I observed my father. Each guest was greeted with enthusiasm, no matter how intrusive the visit might have been. Whether it interrupted him from plans or activities, each person was just as heartily welcomed as those he had been expecting.

It shamed me into silence as I saw how wonderful he always made his guests feel. His home was constantly filled with good feelings and friends who made it a ritual to take time for laughter and love. As I began to adjust to this very social society, I began to see the bondage I was in back home where the open-door policy can be very conditional. What if God asked you to allow someone to live with you for six months without paying rent? Hmm...

There really is no such thing as personal space. All space is a gift from God that has been designated to us for the purpose of sharing with others. The gift of hospitality is one of the most powerful gifts on the planet. As I watched a nation of people opening their doors to those who had lost their homes during the Katrina disaster, I saw the light going on in the faces of the people who had reached out to help. They had found new meaning in their own lives by helping others. I wondered if they even realized why they felt so empowered. This is the supreme expression of love. To give. To give of yourself. To give of what you have that you regard to be a part and extension of yourself. The thing you view as most precious. Your space can be personal, but it shouldn't be. C'mon, give it up. God keeps nothing of Himself back from us. We too should be willing to fling open every door and give access to those He sends to us to nurture.

"But what about boundaries?" you say. "Everyone should have some or people just take advantage of you." It's true they do, but are you willing to chance it in order to have the one rich experience that could change your life? Let's face it. In marriage there really is no such thing as personal space. Someone will be in your space and in your face pretty much all the time for the rest of your life. Not really, but there will be times when it feels like it. How will you share of yourself then if you can't share of yourself now?

Get in the habit of reaching out and pulling someone in. The reason we protect personal space so much really comes from a fear of losing control. Yet when you choose to share your space, you are in control. It's the difference between Christ laying down

His life or others taking it. Though He died, He was in control because He *chose* to lay down His life. When you choose to consider the space you are in an opportunity for being an oasis for others, your world will be filled with the love you longed for all along.

What about your money? You might say, "I worked for it. I earned it. It's mine...isn't it?" All I can say is when I'm talking with singles I hear a whole lot of "I" and "me, me, me" talk and I wonder if these people will ever be able to say "we." It's hard to shift into sharing mode if you haven't practiced. Like the only child who has been indulged for so long but now must share her toy with a visitor, I see many adults hoarding their treasures and pouting when asked to share. If your money belongs to you, you will never have any. "What?" I think just heard a collective yelp. So I will repeat what I just said. If your money is your money, you will never have any. But if your money is *God's* money, He will protect it for you. Keep in mind that we actually do not make a dime without Him. It is He who gives us the power to gain wealth. He then makes us stewards over what we receive.

The mind-set that our money is not our own not only helps us to be more generous people, it also makes us much more responsible. If your money were just yours, you would spend it any ol' kind of way. But when you pause for the cause to consider that God has entrusted a portion of His wealth to you, you must now be more careful of how you manage what has been put in your care. It means that you would distribute it the way He would distribute it. So perhaps that means sacrificing that beautiful sweater you wanted to buy in lieu of helping someone in need. It is profoundly true that our heart is where our treasure is (Matthew 6:21) which is why, in many cases, we put our money, our time, and our efforts where our heart is. And perhaps that is the real issue that needs to be examined.

Exactly where is your heart? Though we are instructed in the Word to guard our heart (Proverbs 4:23), the best way to do that is to surrender your heart to God. Under His protective care it is kept safe from offence, freeing us to walk in love as we should. Are you afraid to love openly? To be vulnerable? Afraid that someone is going to hurt or offend you? Protecting your feelings is the surest way to get them hurt. It is a standing invitation to offence. Consider the irony that people who are shy are often viewed as stuck up or standoffish. The very thing we fear comes upon us because fear is the bait that invites the lion to ravish us. The only thing that saves us from his bite is our ability to surrender all that we are to God along with our expectations of what people should or should not do to us.

If Jesus had protected His feelings, none of us would be redeemed. He literally had to move past His feelings to give Himself for us. He had to press past the rejection, ridicule, betrayal, and abuse and decide to love anyway. This is the nature of God—to love anyway, not on the basis of our response to Him but on the basis of who He is and who He can be for us. Oh, to be like that. To be able to look beyond the faults of people, see their need, and love them in spite of how unlovable they are. To be thin-skinned and easily offended is to be ungodly. That is not walking in love. That is actually making yourself God. Demanding how you should be approached with inflexible rules that others might not be aware of. Your judgment of their actions is the sting that you feel in your own spirit. Oh, the liberty that comes from releasing others to be who they are! It is crucial to your well-being.

In marriage your ability to release your spouse to fail you, to make mistakes, to even offend you will make the difference between celebrating a golden anniversary or agreeing to settle out of court. This is where grace comes into play. The grace to be gracious when others are being graceless. Loving and giving anyway. Determine to walk with open hands and an open heart, trusting God to be your shield and the keeper of your heart. Walk in wisdom but also walk in love, demanding nothing yet inspiring the best in others by being an example of what love looks like.

When we no longer insist on our own way, it frees us to receive everything we want. It actually invites the desires of your heart to come to fruition as others are moved by the liberty you have given to them. Down with self; up with surrender. Sometimes it can be confusing, so remember this simple rule. In the kingdom the way up is down. Give and you shall receive. Crucify self, gain the world. See, it's easy once you die to self. Or as I like to put it, get over yourself.

GETTING REAL

Ce How self-involved are you?

Ce In what area do you feel the greatest sense of entitlement?

Ce In what ways do you make your home available to others in need? Your money? Your time?

Ce What do you fear about being vulnerable?

Ce In what area do you need to surrender more?

Whoever wants to save his life will lose it, but

whoever loses his life for me will save it (Luke 9:24).

JESUS,
breaking down the true cost of selfishness.

MISTAKE
NUMBER EIGHT

*Neglecting the most
important person in your
life next to God—you*

Just thinking out loud...

She stood rooted in awe at her surroundings. The opulence was above and beyond anything she had ever seen before. To think that she, a simple girl, would be standing in the courts of such a powerful king was one thing. To think that she could be chosen to be the next queen was inconceivable! And now his head eunuch stood before her, beckoning her to step closer. With a glint of approval in his eyes, he studied her slowly, as if evaluating every part of her.

It didn't take her long to figure out that she had been given preferential treatment. After ushering her away to a private apartment and giving her a set of personal attendants, the eunuch set about the task of submitting her to a regimen of beauty treatments that other women would only dream about. Baths, lathers, and potions. A special diet. Being fitted for clothing. Training on etiquette and niceties. The art of conversation. She felt as if she were being remade from the inside out. Her quiet time with God became her favorite moments for reflection. Understanding the need to stay grounded in so heady an environment, she clung to her faith with greater fervor than ever before. After all, in spite of what the king decided, she knew her fate was ultimately in God's hands.

As the crown was placed upon her head, Queen Esther also knew that in a world where her king would always have his pick of whatever woman he wanted, the greatest beauty secret she could ever possess would be her relationship with God. (See the book of Esther for Esther's full story.)

In a world where women compete every day for the attention of men, whether from the motive of finding true love or advancement in the marketplace, the beauty contest can be stressful. How does one compete in a world where beauty is purely subjective and driven by media stereotypes? Let's face it. People are not looking at our heart first. Their first impression of you is driven by surface attributes. This can leave a woman feeling very vulnerable. Exactly what is a man—or anyone else, for that matter—looking for? Will you fit the bill? How can you win a contest you never signed up for?

Esther was probably a lot like you, feeling like a fish out of water, or one definitely swimming upstream against the flow of the masses. There will be only one thing that will ultimately separate you from the masses, and it is internal. A beautified spirit reflects on the countenance of a woman giving her a certain *je ne sais quoi*. That "X" factor—something no one can put their finger on—definitely separates the women from the girls. The crowning balance is when we can nurture our insides and outsides in balance so that they complement one another and invite favor from everyone we encounter.

LET'S SELF-EXAMINE

ᐯ What is your greatest beauty asset?

ᐯ What do you think is the thing that attracts others to you?

ᐯ What does your beauty regimen look like?

ᐯ What type of physical shape are you in? How is your health?

ᐯ What is the greatest hindrance to you being your best? What are you going to do about it?

Solution: Take care of yourself

Everyone longs for love, but for various and sundry reasons. Some want to have someone to shower affection and service over. Others long for someone to complete them, to literally fill in the blank spots of their lives, to be what they are not...watch out! This is an unhealthy motive. The commandments tell us to love our neighbor as we love ourselves. Ephesians 5:28 encourages, "In this same way, husbands ought to love their wives as their own bodies. He who loves his wife loves himself." I find it interesting that women have to be taught how to love their husbands while the men are simply commanded to do so. Perhaps that's another book. However, the umbrella theme is that one must have a healthy heart condition in order to love others the way God loves us. God not only loves us, He loves Himself. Not egotistically, but in the sense that He knows what He has to offer to us and why we should want it. As long as you don't love yourself, you will always feel unworthy of getting the love you desire. Therefore, it is important to take good care of yourself first in order to be able to reach out to others freely.

The instructions given on the plane for those who find themselves in an emergency situation are to first put the oxygen mask over your own face before attempting to help anyone else. Why?

Because you have to live long enough to help the person next to you! This would require you being in prime condition. The point I'm trying to make is it is impossible to love someone else the way God has designed us to love until we love ourselves. While charity begins at home, so does love.

The manifestation of how we see ourselves usually plays out in our physical appearance as well as the things we do or don't do to promote personal well-being. So let's take a look at the areas that are crucial requirements for approaching love and loving from a healthy place. Of course, none of us have the luxury of the lush world that Esther found herself in. I know that none of us are getting massages on a daily basis as part of our regular regimen, but there are things that we can do to promote wholeness within ourselves that radiates a beauty that won't be bowed by the competition because there will be no competition.

First beauty secret—take time to nurture your spirit. The ultimate love you will ever experience will be between yourself and the One who created you and loves you most. Your Abba Father, Father God, and the Lover of your soul, the soon-coming Bridegroom, Jesus Himself. As His best man, the person of the Holy Spirit reveals His heart and His words to you. No sweeter love can be found. In His arms is where you are safe to surrender completely to love, to being vulnerable, to being open to all He longs to pour into you.

Here is where you learn of unselfishness, servanthood, patience, kindness, and all the things you long to experience in a relationship. This is the One who says what He means and means what He says. The only One completely capable of being faithful and true, of never leaving you or forsaking you. Here is where you will learn of consistency and grace. Forgiveness and mercy again and again as you continually fail Him and yet He never fails you. Oh, yes. If you want to learn something about love, you had better get with the One who *invented* love!

Here is where you get to practice intimacy without fearing any rejection or repercussions. You can be open and vulnerable, sharing your deepest feelings and fears, hurts, and questions. In His arms you are safe. If you can't be transparent with God, how can you bare yourself to anyone else? Your ability to enjoy your love relationship will be in direct proportion to your ability to share yourself in love with your heavenly Fiancé.

How do you approach Him? Do you spend quality time with Him? Listening, seeking His face, searching His heart, reading His Word? Or do you go looking for someone else or something else to fill the void that only He can fill? When we draw near to Him, reveling in His love for us, we find ourselves filled with love to overflowing. This overflow is what we give to others. When we are dry, we start from a place of deficit, which means we really have nothing left to give. This is why our expectancy is turned toward someone we think can give us something we don't have. We find ourselves disappointed because, chances are, they were empty too and have nothing to give... or not enough to give. It's never enough if we rely on human love to fill us up. God did not design us with the ability to fill each other. He left a space in us that only He can fill. Until we surrender to this very profound fact, we will exist in perpetual disappointment, losing hope that love will ever be the all in all we long for it to be.

Take the time to feed and refresh your spirit daily. Talk to God. Then take the time to listen. Journal, writing down what you hear. Read His Word. Reflect on what it means to you personally. Decide what you are going to do with what you have read. Worship. Set the mood with music and enter into His presence. Lose yourself in praise to Him. Cry, even. Let your tears wash you and refresh you. You pick the time. You pick the place. Only meet Him there, and let Him do what no one else can do—beautify you.

Starting from the inside out is important, but one without the other just won't do. God wants us to take care of our bodies. At times I think we are prone to spiritualizing our appearance. We feel that if we are being good little Christian boys and girls, our one vice of overeating or not taking proper care of our bodies is permissible. Yet the body is the temple God lives in (1 Corinthians 3:16). Our temples should glorify Him just as the physical building that King Solomon built in honor of Him did. I believe it is safe to say that not being or looking your physical best is not proof of your spirituality, but actually a lack of it. We should not rely on our outward beauty, but we certainly do God a disservice if we don't choose to represent Him by being excellent in our appearance.

You are the only Jesus someone may see, so don't make Him look tacky. Whether you are a size 2 or a 22, be the best you that you can be. Your appearance is just as important to you as it is to those who see you, because you will telegraph how you feel about yourself to those around you. If you are not looking your best, you will not feel good about yourself, and this will bear out in the way you carry yourself and interact with others. This can have an effect on the relationship you are seeking to initiate, as well as preexisting friendships and associations. If we don't love ourselves, it is difficult to love and celebrate others.

Negativity sets in when we don't have a good view of ourselves. This is usually driven by the thought that we are not up to par in our own minds. Some of this can be a bit obsessive, but I'm speaking of realistic terms. When I know I'm overweight, not only does my body feel bad and my clothing fit poorly, but my countenance reflects all of my ill feelings. Insecurity is more prevalent, and I find myself unable to be as open as when I am celebrating feeling on top of my body instead of being ruled by it. Are you getting my drift?

Sometimes we are our own worst enemy and the greatest repellent to the love that we so deeply desire. It's time to take a good look in the mirror and your closet. Perhaps you don't need to go any further than listening to your body with all its aches and pains. Those aches and pains are cries for help, saying, "Please stop eating that way. Please give me some exercise. Please give me some rest!"

Now, I know I just messed with somebody. Can we talk about rest? I believe a lot of times the reason we abuse our bodies is because we are not giving it the rest it needs. When the body is rested, it requires less food. Less food in balance allows the body to do the work it needs to do to burn and absorb calories and nutrients in a more efficient manner, thus giving the body a greater degree of natural energy that does not burn us out. Yet we push ourselves to the limit and sedate ourselves with all the wrong types of food to fake energy, which actually makes us more tired. Anyone exhausted yet? Or how about just plain ol' depressed? Yup, that is usually what happens. Most of us eat an array of foods that totally throws our system off balance, overloading us with sugar and other things that have a chemical effect on not only our body but also our emotions. Small wonder we're falling apart and feeling even worse about ourselves. Again, if we don't love ourselves, who will? How can you convince someone you are a worthwhile investment if you don't feel that way yourself?

Perhaps the deeper issue you might not want to deal with is what you really are hungry for…if you struggle with overeating.

Spiritual hunger can mask itself as physical hunger. When we are low on intimacy with God, the void in our heart begins to signal that something is missing. This can manifest in lots of different ways, from shopoholism to looking for love in all the wrong places to probably what most view as the safest way of anesthetizing emptiness and discomfort—eating or some other form of oral fixation that wreaks havoc on our bodies. The worse our bodies feel, the worse we feel emotionally and spiritually. Truly, it is a chain reaction. God invites us to eat His Word and be filled. "Listen to me and eat what is good and let your soul delight itself in fatness." I'm paraphrasing Isaiah 55:2. Another translation states that your soul will delight in the richest of fare. A full soul will not feel the need to go looking for crumbs of immediate gratification or empty fillers, which are like empty calories. They do nothing beneficial for our bodies or our psyche. Perhaps it's time to answer a hard question. What are you really hungry for?

Take the time to examine your body and take note of how you can be kinder to it. Be honest about the things you submit it to that are damaging. Walk in accountability with someone who can help you get on the right track. Go for a walk. Take an exercise class. Just get moving! Examine the things you eat and be honest with yourself about what you need to set aside. This is the only body you are going to get, so treat it with care. Sometimes we treat temporal possessions better than we treat our bodies. How can you take care of someone else well if you don't take care of yourself well? Those same bad eating habits are what you will bring to your marriage, except now you will be cooking for two or more. Don't contribute to the bad health of your spouse and your children. Remember, it is never just about you. Though it is your body, its state of health will affect others.

Your emotional health is last but certainly not least in the scenario of taking care of yourself. You alone are responsible for your heart; no one else. The Bible tells you to guard your heart with all diligence because the issues of life flow out of it (Proverbs 4:23). That would include love. It is up to you to make choices that nurture a healthy heart condition. One free from unforgiveness, bitterness, pride, jealousy, envy, and strife along with the rest of the works of the flesh that all manifest from a bad state of heart.

Here is where you must take the time for introspection. The Bible tells us that certain emotional states affect us physically. There have been testimonies of people who were afflicted with cancer or on their deathbeds from other illnesses being revived and healed from immersing themselves in laughter therapy. The Scriptures say it all: "A cheerful heart is good medicine, but a crushed spirit dries up the bones" (Proverbs 17:22). "An anxious heart weighs a man down" (Proverbs 12:25). "Hope deferred makes the heart sick, but a longing fulfilled is a tree of life" (Proverbs 13:12). "A heart at peace gives life to the body, but envy rots the bones" (Proverbs 14:30). "A cheerful look brings joy to the heart, and good news gives health to the bones" (Proverbs 15:30). Do these verses convince you that your health is very much a matter to take to heart? We can literally become heartsick! The condition of our emotions can have a profound effect on our personal health. It is all intermarried. The root eventually affects the fruit. You are a spirit-being possessing a soul that makes its home in your body. Though these are separately addressed, they are not separate in function. One feeds the energy and the well-being of the other.

Our physical maladies can sometimes be hard to locate if we live in denial of how we really feel. Small wonder that the number of stress-related diseases has risen. In honor of your temple, but most importantly God and yourself, you need to take the time to be in touch with yourself emotionally. Facing your feelings head-on and sharing them with someone you can trust to help you process them properly is vital to your good health. Your feelings of fear, disappointment, frustration, being overwhelmed, depression—whatever—are not an indication of a lack of faith. God acknowledges that we will be assaulted by our emotions as we go through the rigors of day-to-day life fraught with all its dramas and surprises. It's what we do with our emotions that concerns Him. This is why He says, " 'Be angry, and do not sin': do not let the sun go down on your wrath" (Ephesians 4:29 NKJV). Or, "Weeping may endure for a night, but joy comes in the morning" (Psalm 30:5 NKJV). God never chastises anyone for experiencing the emotions they have because He too has wept. He too has been angry. He simply desires that we master our responses and emotions and don't allow them to rule over us to the point that they affect our health or cause us to make bad choices that could affect the quality of our life.

David, king of Israel, was quick to say what was bothering him in his psalms. He was not a man in denial; he would end his dissertation of what he knew to be true in spite of the circumstances with what God was able to do. He chose to keep hope alive no matter how dire his circumstances or how overwhelmed and out of control he was feeling. We should also choose the outlet of honesty and transparency with ourselves, God, and others in our inner circle. Accountability helps us to keep our accounts short. Not allowing issues and emotions to build up over time keeps us free from the outbursts that can occur when things are left unresolved. Keep in mind that whatever is already within us is what comes out when we are squeezed. Our responses and reactions are merely the reflection of our heart condition. "As water reflects a face, so a [woman's] heart reflects the [woman]" (Proverbs 27:19). Let's be honest. You can spot a person who has issues a mile away by their countenance. Our eyes give us away; perhaps this is where the saying "the eyes are the windows to the soul" came from. They betray bitterness, fear, anger, you name it. No amount of makeup or accessories can mask what they reveal.

It is important to be responsible for the gifts God has given you. Your body and everything about you is a gift. Treat yourself as the precious gift you are. You've been given one body, one heart, and one mind. They are the only ones you are going to get, so maintain them well and they will work for you and champion you through life. They will also transform you into a vessel that honors God and glorifies Him in the eyes of others. A well-kept woman is always a reflection of how well her lover has taken care of her. Show the world what an amazing provider the Lover of your soul is by looking like a cherished vessel.

Learn the secret of true beauty and make your personal toilette complete with natural beautifiers—love, joy, and peace. These come from a heart at rest, free from all that could bind it. A body that is sound. Emotions that are in balance. A spirit that is surrendered to God and full of His wisdom, assurances, and promises. This is beauty from the inside out. The kind that surpasses the ravages of wear and lasts a lifetime.

GETTING REAL

What are you really hungry for?

What have been the greatest hindrances to your sense of well-being?

How do you feel about your spiritual health? What can you do to improve this area?

How do you feel about yourself physically? What realistic steps can you take to improve this area?

What is your emotional state? What things are areas of concerns? How will you address them?

Do you not know that your body is a temple of

the Holy Spirit, who is in you, whom you have

received from God? You are not your own; you

were bought at a price. Therefore honor God

with your body (1 Corinthians 6:19-20).

THE APOSTLE PAUL,
dealing with a society who put the emphasis on
all the wrong things for the wrong reasons.

*Subjecting your heart
to foolish choices*

Just thinking out loud...

He had been here before. It was the same woman. Only the name and the face had changed. The same lies, the same manipulation and deceit, were very much a repeat performance of his past relationships. And yet he was clueless. He didn't see the impending disaster creeping into his life like a slow fog over the horizon of his understanding. As he stood flexing his muscles, confident of his ability to free himself from his latest bondage, he realized that this time the same old game he always played had played out. Fresh out of grace, he found himself facing the consequences of all his former choices. Choices he refused to take responsibility for or examine. And now it had come to this. Cruelly blinded by his captors and tied up like an animal, his disgrace was complete as the woman he loved watched him being carried away in contempt.

Bound in his heart as well as in physical chains, he sat in darkness, contemplating his future while regretting his past. Why had it taken so long for him to see the error of his ways, all the wrong choices? Why had he allowed his flesh to drown out the voice of his spirit? How could he have gotten so far off track, throwing away a promising future in favor of temporary passion and fleeting moments of pleasure? Now the irrevocable and lasting price seemed far too high to pay for something that had once seemed like innocent fun. No harm done, he had thought, until this. Now he would never fulfill his destiny. Never live up to the call God had placed on his life. Never be able to regain his former stature. After all he had done for his people, the only thing anyone would ever remember about Samson was his demise at the hands of Delilah. In one last valiant effort to redeem himself, Samson killed more Philistines in one fell swoop than he had during his entire career as a judge in Israel. Unfortunately, he died among the rubble of the stadium along with his enemies. But perhaps he had died inside much earlier than that fateful day. (Look again at Samson's story in Judges 16.)

We all die in degrees every time we make a poor choice that subjects our hearts to far more wear and tear than they were designed to take. The pursuit of immediate pleasure can be overwhelming, especially in light of an uncertain future. Will we ever really find someone who will love us the way we long to be loved? What if Mr. Right never comes along? Would it be so wrong to settle for Mr. He'll Do? Peer pressure pushes us to keep up appearances (against our better judgment in some instances), and in the silence of our rooms when our tears have washed away the rose-colored glaze, we look at our shattered expectations lying around us and wonder what went wrong. We, like Samson, need to be introspective and own our part in the dramas that can play out in our lives in the area of romantic relationships. This is the only way to break unhealthy patterns and begin to move forward with wise heart choices. It is mind over heart matters whether we want to do the work or not. The truth that must be faced is that using our head is the only way to experience victory in the love department.

LET'S GET DOWN TO THE NITTY-GRITTY

ℂ What patterns have you seen emerging in your love life?

ℂ What type of man are you attracted to?

ℂ Are your romantic choices conducive to getting the committed relationship you seek?

ℂ What choices have you made in the past that you presently regret?

ℂ What will you do differently next time?

Solution: Get heart-smart

I find it very interesting that one of the leading causes of death among women, even greater than breast cancer, is heart disease. This is not just a physical fact. I believe it is a spiritual fact as well. We are told by the Word of God that the heart harbors all things that affect, concern, or relate to life (Proverbs 4:23). "Hope deferred makes the heart sick" (Proverbs 13:12), and the disease can spread throughout our entire system. So let's talk about ways to safeguard our hearts and our wholeness so that we can be free to love as God has created us to love and experience the joy He wants us to.

I decided to take a brief survey among various groups of people before writing this book. I asked, "What do you think are the top ten mistakes singles make?" Consistently the answers were the same. The conversation went something like this: "Well, women give away too much too soon." "They compromise their standards in the area of purity." "They end up settling for far less than the best man for them." "They don't allow the man to pursue them." "They get attached to relationships that are not going anywhere." On and on, virtually every comment was about how women handled relationships. The rest of life was completely ignored. This is the reason I placed this area close to the last because you could not possibly be heart-smart without clearing up the other business we've walked through first. Hopefully by now you've laid a better foundation with the other things we've discussed and can now put these principles to use. Because this chapter could actually be a book by itself, I will refer you to several other books I have written that deal with this subject more specifically. *Ending the Search for Mr. Right, Secrets of an Irresistible Woman, If Men Are Like Buses, Then How Do I Catch One?* and *The Unspoken Rules of Love* will give you additional insight into the things you need to know to walk in wisdom in the area of your interpersonal relationships. For now I will tackle several of the top issues and leave you to do additional research should you need to.

You see, all the above-mentioned behavior is merely the fruit and not the root of why we do what we do. When our hearts are healthy, we don't tolerate bad behavior from others or place our hearts in precarious positions. When we allow ourselves to be transformed by the power of God's Word and are yielding to His clear direction, we begin to attract not only different people but different circumstances into our midst. Far too many women walk with open hands when it comes to matters of the heart. Or worse yet, they toss their heart into the air, hoping someone responsible will catch it. When it lands with a thud, damaged before us, we blame others for not taking better care of it.

Let me ask you a question. Where do you leave your good jewelry? Do you leave it out on the coffee table in the middle of the living room? If you knew some strangers were coming to your home for a party, would you leave your valuables out where they could be stolen? I didn't think so.

Well, the same rule applies to your heart, so here we go with the countdown of ten mistakes we most often make once we think we've met the "man of our dreams."

GETTING REAL

- What has been the repetitive pattern in all of your relationships? What can you do differently to break this pattern?

- In what areas do you wish you had been smarter in your previous relationships?

- What happens when your heart gets ahead of your head? What is the outcome of your actions?

- What would you like to be more in control of in your relationships? What makes you out of control now?

Number One: Use Your Heads, Ladies

The one thing you must remember is that when God asks us to love Him, He instructs us to love Him with all our heart, soul, mind, and strength (Mark 12:30). Yes, the mind is involved because our emotions should follow our decisions, not the other way around. After the mind has committed to loving Him, then the emotions are engaged and maintained through the strength of our convictions, which are reinforced by our belief and trust in Him.

The same is true when it comes to dealing with a natural man, except it is now more important to engage our intellect for a different reason. Remember, the heart can deceive you and mislead you. Based on what your heart wants, it will twist words and circumstances to conform to its desires. This is where many women fool themselves into guessing a man's intentions and then find themselves deeply disappointed when they discover their assumptions were not correct.

Relationships affect every area of our well-being and how we respond to people and circumstances at large. Someone who is heartbroken is not whole. When we are broken, it is hard to walk in a godly manner. Our inability to walk as God has created us and called us to affects our overall victory. The outcome of our interpersonal relationships have a profound effect on how we see ourselves.

Based on acceptance or rejection, we absorb a view of ourselves that can make it hard for us to function in a healthy manner, thereby affecting our work, our personal care of ourselves, and our overall response to everything that occurs in our world, from a light turning red to a salesclerk being rude, which in turn invites a response in us that either affirms us as being of value or confirms our greatest fears about ourselves—that we are not enough; therefore, we are unworthy of love. God wants us to walk in wholeness and that wholeness cannot be determined by another person, but it can be affected by him if you are not using your head in your romantic or platonic interactions. When we don't use our head, we set ourselves up for disappointment by not paying attention to key signs that let us know what our expectations of the other person ought or ought not to be. Having realistic expectations is a haven to a healthy heart. "Hope deferred makes the heart sick, but a longing fulfilled is a tree of life" (Proverbs 13:12). The responsibility of your heart being kept in prime condition is solely yours. So take good care of it. Though resilient, your heart can affect every area of your well-being if subjected to too many unnecessary traumas. You don't need a bunch of men in your life...just the right one for you. When you choose to utilize discernment, you will be able to make more sound choices for successful living and loving.

GETTING REAL

ℭ In what ways do you set yourself up for heartache?

ℭ How has allowing your emotions to rule over your good judgment caused problems for you in the past?

ℭ What are the first signs for you that you are letting your heart overrule your better judgment?

ℭ What is a situation when you were heart-smart that you feel good about? What was the outcome?

Number Two: Leave the Pursuing to the Man

This is huge, ladies. This one principle will save you much unnecessary heartache. I understand there is a new breed of woman out there. One who is self-assured, independent, and in control of her world. I say if you're that self-assured, you can be sure that a man will see your worth and pursue you. You will be independent enough not to make desperate moves that will cost you later because you are not desperate for a man—you would just like to have one. And you will be in control of your impulses above all things because you are using your head when it comes to men. I am not trying to be harsh, but I feel strongly that this is a dangerous practice that often ends in heartbreak. Please, ladies, take better care of your heart! It is scripturally out of order for a woman to pursue a man. If you don't believe in Scripture, then let me say it is universal law. God's Word works whether you believe it or not. Men are created and wired to pursue. Women were created to be the cherished prize. We lose status and value in their eyes when we do the pursuing. When I was growing up, women used to advise their daughters, "You need to marry a man who loves you more than you love him." I used to think that was terrible advice. They advised this because they felt that if the man loved the woman more than she loved him, their daughter would never be hurt. In a way, that is true.

If we look at spiritual order, we love because Jesus first loved us. He is the ultimate model of the Bridegroom in the Spirit, which should translate to the natural. The man should choose you as Christ chose us. He should pursue you, fight for you, and win you, just as Christ has done for us.

I always get asked the question, "Well, what if the man is shy, Michelle, or has been hurt by someone else and needs a little help?" My answer will always be the same. No man is too shy when it comes to going after something he wants. If he is passive about pursuing you, he will be passive about other things that are important to you as well—such as pursuing employment, promotion, or anything that would move your life together forward. You will become the principle decision-maker at your house and eventually run out of respect and desire for him because you are tired of wearing the pants in the relationship. You will push his buttons forever to validate if he truly loves you because you will never have the peace that comes from the knowledge that he chose you. This becomes the devil's playground as he constantly challenges and questions you with a little voice that whispers, "Are you sure you are his first choice?" Don't put yourself in this position.

What is the balance on this topic? Be approachable but don't do the approaching. Does this mean you can say hello? Of course. Compliment him on his tie if you like. Just don't put the moves on him. Your job is to make him know it's safe to approach you. His job is to invite you out and do the work it takes to get to know you better. A simple mantra for you to remember is this: Your job is to be. His job is to do. Got it? As I've written before, pretend you are a flower. What does a flower do? It just sits there looking and smelling pretty. It doesn't shout out to be picked. It is what it is and those who recognize its beauty choose to take it home and set it in a place where it can be appreciated most.

Allowing yourself to be chosen is one of the ways that you guard your heart. When you are the prize that man is after, your value increases in his eyes. He knows that he must do the work to secure the relationship. Your attention and time are not taken for granted because he remembers that he had to earn your interest. When you do the choosing, you set yourself up to be replaced by the one that he desires to pursue. In his mind he did not choose you; he was chosen and therefore settled for someone who was not quite what he would have chosen for himself. Therefore, when he sees someone who is more in line with what he had in mind, whether that person is actually a better choice for him or not, he will pursue her. You've heard the stories of women dating a man for two or three years, and he then breaks up with her and marries someone else after knowing them for only three months. There can be several explanations for this, but one of the main ones is who chose whom... Nuff said.

GETTING REAL

ce What is your rationale for pursuing a man? How has this worked for you?

ce How do you feel when a man is the one in pursuit of you?

ce Can you compare your level of confidence between when you pursue and when you are pursued? Which one feels better? Why?

Number Three: Ask the Right Questions

He just approached you, the man of your dreams. He's tall, dark, and handsome. He's successful, he's got a great sense of humor, and he likes you! But what else about him? What do you really know about this person? If you've been starving for male attention for some time, his attention might be enough for you—but it shouldn't be. You need to find out if he deserves your excitement. It amazes me how many people get caught up in romance and forget about the practical aspects of life they will have to deal with after the rose-colored hue has faded from their eyes and they land back in the real world of everyday living.

What goals does he have? Do they match yours? What is his idea of living a good life? This is important. He might be a country boy at heart while you are a city girl. So when he wants to move to the outskirts of town, you will not be a happy camper. Now is the time to learn of his likes and dislikes. The things that are important to him. What his priorities are in life.

What does his idea of a good relationship look like? What does he expect from the woman in his life? These types of things are important to know. You want to know if he values women. Does he have definite ideas about the gender roles? What does he want his life to look like in five years? Ten? Twenty? You might be surprised to find that his idea of a fabulous life does or does not match yours.

Does he want children? BIG question! If he doesn't want children and you do, this is a deal breaker. He will not change his mind and will only resent you for going against his wishes should you choose to have a child anyway—if you make it to the altar. Or perhaps you do not want children and he does. He will resent you for not giving him what he wants. Now is not the time to think you can marry the man today and change his ways tomorrow. People are who they are, and they have made decisions about what they want and like according to years of conditioning. These types of things do not change overnight, if they change at all. In light of the fact that you would want your wishes honored, you must do the same with the man in your life and not discount his opinion or feelings. This is why it is important to find out the answers to the things that matter most to you to see if you are a good fit for one another.

What else is important to you? Cleanliness? Frugal money sense? A love of the arts and music? Travel? Close family ties? An extensive social life? Good fashion sense? A neat home? The list goes on and on of things that you don't discover as being really important to you until after you've said "I do." The fallout of being irritated by the other person's lack of commitment to what is important to you can cause major problems later. Now is the time to locate what your needs are for a joyful and healthy life. These are things to discuss as you have dinner or enjoy an outing in a casual setting that is not threatening. People love to talk about themselves, so it should not be difficult to get the answers you need to know.

Yes, even potential relationships should have an interview. Jobs do, and marriage is the most difficult job you will ever be called to master. Just as no boss hires an employee who is not qualified to do the job, you should not consider someone for lifetime partnership who doesn't fit the bill of your desires or needs. Though opposites attract, commonalities are the glue that assist a relationship in remaining intact for the long-term. The Word of God asks the question, "Can two walk together, unless they are agreed?" (Amos 3:3 NKJV).

I know I don't have to tell anyone reading this book that one of the most important areas you must address is the area of your spirituality. You cannot be unequally yoked in this area (2 Corinthians 6:14). Many have tried and had miserable results when they found themselves always attending church alone or arguing over the basics, such as prayer and tithing, because one person is committed to living a submitted life before God and the other person is not. This becomes a major problem as the woman tries to get her man to line up with her vision of what his spiritual walk should look like.

Depending on how a sister handles this one, the rift can either close up or blow up. Remember, Jesus is your only high priest. Your husband will be just a man in need of a Savior just like you. The key is to find out what his heart is toward God before you take the blind leap into his arms or the sea of love. His love life with God will become more important to you than you presently think. Keep in mind that a man who doesn't want to break God's heart won't break yours, either. To have a man who knows he is accountable to God for how he treats you is a tremendous blessing. That being said, just because someone says they are a Christian doesn't mean it is necessarily so. Again, actions speak louder than words here. There is no need to be judgmental, though you do need to be clear that you have specific standards for the man who gets to insert himself into your life. Then leave the choice open to him of where he wants to fit into your life. If he wants you enough, he will do whatever it takes to be with you, including living his faith in Christ. If he uses the old "You need to accept me as I am" line, release him to go on his way nicely but firmly. You must be on the same spiritual page in order to fully enjoy the book of marriage.

Of course, you must be cognizant of the different levels of your friendship and know when it is right to ask certain questions. Because, believe me, there are some difficult questions you need to ask at some juncture. They aren't the most comfortable things to probe into, but again, you don't need any unwelcome surprises.

In the world we live in today you must ask a man if he's ever experimented with other men sexually. Again, this line of questioning is only appropriate if he is seeming to be romantically intentional toward you. With the "down-low" phenomenon looming ever larger and women contracting HIV/AIDS by the droves, we must be heart-smart. Is he willing to take a test before you move forward to a deeper relationship? Though you have no intention of being sexually involved until marriage, this is still information you need to know if he is serious about courting you with marriage in mind.

The state of finances is another difficult conversation to have at times, but it must be had so that decisions can be made. Sometimes it's best to wait until large amounts of debt have been taken care of before joining yourself to someone who might come to resent inheriting a mountain of monies owed.

I think you've got the picture. Make a list of what is important to you. What you want your marriage to look like, your relationship to look like, and ask the questions that line up with those trains of thought to make sure you are both wanting the same things out of life. Remember, romance wears off and real life sets in quick, fast, and in a hurry, and if both people agree on where they are going, the journey will be a whole lot sweeter!

GETTING REAL

ℭ Make a list of the character traits that are important to you in your life partner.

ℭ How good are you at asking a potential suitor questions?

ℭ What keeps you from asking the hard questions? How has this been harmful in the past?

ℭ What issues are important to you for your future? How important is it for you to ask about these areas? Why?

Number Four: Keep Your Mystery

I'm not talking about playing games, ladies. I'm talking about the type of mystery that puts things on a man's mind and leaves him wanting more of you. No one deserves to have all of you right away. Part of the delight of receiving flowers is watching how much more beautiful they become as they open in increments day by day, their fragrance growing sweeter as they unfold. We need to learn a lesson from those flowers.

Now that I've told you to ask all the right questions, you need to know the right things to tell. I'm a sister, you're a sister, but let me tell you, sister, that for the most part women talk way too much and give up way too much too soon! What is it? Do you really believe that if you let this man know all the ways you've been hurt before that he will be moved to protect you more? It just does not work that way. Let me tell you what he's thinking. "Hmm...if all these other men treated her this way, what was it they saw that I might be missing?" Or "Why did she allow herself to be treated that way? She must not feel she deserves to be treated any better, and perhaps she doesn't!" The more you expose, the more questions it will raise in his mind that will not cast you in a good light.

The other part of this equation is that men don't like to hear about other men. Whether they will admit it or not, they rather fancy the notion of being THE man in your life. They do not savor being on the list. And if the former men on your list are being discussed in such great detail, either your current man will be worried about lingering feelings you may harbor for your past love or believe that at some point in time you will be discussing him with someone else. That is not something he would appreciate. My simple rule on this is unless there is something that has occurred in your life romantically or health-wise that will have impact on your current relationship, keep it to yourself.

If you feel the need to still nurse and rehearse whatever the matter may be, it is safe to say that you have not been healed in that area, and this is a conversation you need to take to the Lord so that He can restore you. To unload information that is not your potential suitors' business is TMI (too much information). Let's approach this in reverse. Do you really want to hear all of the gory details about his other girlfriends? I didn't think so. You should want to know just enough of his history to know if he is a commitment-phobe or if he has a pattern of blaming others when things don't work out versus owning his part of whatever occurred. But intimate details about how his heart was kicked to the curb and how he agonized over someone other than you? I think not.

Many have asked me what determines something as being too much information, and my answer is simply this: Anything you don't want filed in the back of someone's mind for future leverage. Anything you don't want to revisit again during happier times. Anything you don't want held against you. Anything you don't want used as emotional blackmail or a tool of manipulation. Are you getting this?

Here is the other guideline for choosing what to divulge. What is your motive for sharing this bit of information? Is it to garner sympathy? To create some sort of strange bond that feels like intimacy because you shared a secret? To shock the person? To get them to open up? These are all the wrong reasons for sharing information. You do not want to illicit feelings of sympathy from your potential suitor. You want to inspire feelings of warmth and endearment, romantic thoughts, and longing for more time with you.

The way to do this effectively is to take cues from him and follow his lead. This means you must be more interested in him than in revealing yourself to him. Because people love to talk about themselves, the more questions you ask him about himself, the more he will feel you are truly interested in him. This is a good thing. As he shares things with you, feel free to share experiences and thoughts that coincide with what he is sharing. This builds a natural bridge of commonality between you that paves the way for friendship and understanding that can ultimately lead to romance if he feels he has enough in common with you and vice versa. This is the natural and healthy way to build a lasting bond that can move toward intimacy.

The other way you can preserve your mystery and leave him wanting more is in the way you present yourself physically. Less is not more when it comes to clothing unless we are talking about accessories. Your power lies in what he does not see, my sister. Every man likes to think of his woman as his greatest secret. A garden that only he can explore. He does not like to share all his woman's wares with the rest of the world. Though the world has bought into the concept that the more they show the more attention they will attract, might I submit to you that not all attention is good attention.

As a woman of God, modesty is not just a sign of godliness—it can be downright sexy! It is what is in the package that counts. The way you carry yourself with an easy confidence. In tasteful, stylish outfits that always pique the interest and leave one guessing. Possess yourself and know you are a gift that will be unwrapped at the right time but not a moment before. That is why it is important for you to have your own sources of delight beyond that man. Leave the question on his mind as to why you are so self-satisfied and joyful.

It's the little things that create mystery, from the way you laugh to the way you smell—it's called being provocative without being lascivious. It is all about being naturally you and delighting in being who you are. This is the gift that God has given to every woman that the world tries to exploit, but as we learn the power behind it we reclaim the pieces of ourselves and learn to share them sparingly until someone deserves to receive an overflow. Until then, store all things precious where they can be safe.

GETTING REAL

ᴄᴇ What are special things about you others have taken note of that you take for granted?

ᴄᴇ In what ways do you give too much of yourself too soon? What prompts you to do this? What is the outcome when you do this?

ᴄᴇ What unresolved matters do you find yourself repeating that need to be healed in your heart before you move on?

ᴄᴇ In what ways can you preserve your mystery?

Number Five: Don't Ignore the Signs!

When you know your value, you won't fall for the okeydoke. That would be the games men can play with your heart. Smart women listen as well as take note of the actions that follow. Let's begin with words. Actions do speak louder than words, but you must also know when to pay attention to what is being said. When a man says things like, "I don't deserve you" or "You are too good for me" believe him! Don't try to change his mind. You will only find out later that he was absolutely right.

God allows us to hear and see what we need to in order to give us the opportunity to save ourselves from future heartache, but usually we are so caught up in the euphoria of having the prospect of romance that we ignore the waving red flags and proceed without caution. Bad move. If a man says, "I am not ready for a commitment," the true translation is, "I'm not ready for a commitment with you." Don't get mad. Thank him for his honesty and either place him in the friendship file or move on if you know that you will not be able to spend time with him without your expectations for more being raised.

So what's a girl to think if he is saying all the right things but his actions don't match? If he doesn't keep his word before the wedding, he most certainly will not keep it after you've said your vows. His actions are the true reflection of his heart. "As he thinketh in his heart, so is he" (Proverbs 23:8 KJV). If he wants to be with you, he will be by your side without you having to ask.

Moving on. Trust must be earned. Actions always speak louder than words. If he is talking out loud but doing nothing to back up his vocal good intentions, don't invest your heart. Far too many women give away their hearts before a man has proven himself worthy of receiving it.

Hear this, ladies. Men have patterns and they cannot be

ignored. A man will always start off hot and heavy when he is in active pursuit. If you allow yourself to be caught too soon, he will cool off even faster than he pursued you, so it is up to you to pace the relationship. Don't be so readily available from the beginning. Give him the space and the time to become intentional toward you.

After you've settled into a groove, however, it is up to you to take note of his personal pattern of interaction with you. If anything about it changes, you must take note of the change. Disappearing acts are never acceptable. If you cannot account for large chunks of time in his schedule and he remains elusive, beware. He either has unfinished business elsewhere or business *he is not going to finish* elsewhere, and either of these answers disqualifies him from your consideration as a love interest. A man who harbors secrets and is not forthcoming about his whereabouts is not operating in integrity toward you. In this day and age, his secrecy could be a matter of life or death for you.

If he keeps you a secret, don't ignore the red flags. A man who truly sees you as his woman and someone he is investing himself in wants to expose you to his inner circle and all who are important to him. He is transparent about his association with you. While you are dating, this is the time to learn everything about him that you possibly can. You will never totally know someone until you are living with them, but you can do your homework beforehand and lessen the number of surprises.

If he doesn't exhibit manners and consideration now, he never will. This is a part of his character and who he is. If he is stingy versus frugal, check that now and don't be surprised when he shows no interest in indulging you with the things that you like to be showered with. If he starts off taking more than he gives, don't overlook these tendencies. They are little markers you need to pay attention to.

I've said it often that dating is not for mating; it is for collecting data. This is the time you are checking him out to see if he even *qualifies* for more serious consideration. This is where you pull out that lovely list you submitted to God when you were putting in your order for a mate and begin to cross-check it between what you've written and what is being manifested before your very eyes. Your list should have a countdown of realistic expectations beyond surface traits that will eventually fade.

There are many qualifiers that must be examined before you can feel free to give your heart away. The ultimate goal is to not only marry your best friend, but a man of upstanding character. This takes time and lots of communication before you make the decision to move forward.

Chemistry is a temporary sonic blast at best. After the smoke clears there had better be a real man standing there. Real men keep their promises. They consider your heart, your time, your spirit. They seek to protect you and cover you. A real man interested in you will want to know everything about you. He will note what is important to you and look for ways to please and support you. He will be like Jesus to you, giving himself for your sake.

What type of things are you to be taking note of? The way he speaks about his family and other women—especially his mother. This will reveal how he feels about women. Unresolved issues with his mother are not good. Be wise—those issues will be superimposed over you. If he is a mama's boy, this has to be examined; you could end up being the other woman if he is not able to keep his relationship with his mother in proper perspective. Take a look at his family dynamics. That could be your family in a few years. What kind of family life has he been exposed to? A healthy or dysfunctional one? What is his normal? Is it normal to you? All of these things need to be soberly considered. After all, this is the rest of your life we are talking about.

His friends and his job history are other key indicators. His friends are like him, so examine them closely. Are they disrespectful and morally loose or godly, successful, and considerate? Whatever they are, he is like that when he is not around you. Birds of a feather still flock together, the last time I checked. The length of his association with his friends and his job will tell you how he deals with long-term commitment. If his life is a revolving door, this is a serious indicator of things to come.

How does he handle his emotions as well as his money? Two other biggies. Anger management is a big one to check out. The indicators of potential abuse are usually apparent before two people walk down the aisle. The mistake most women make is to assume they can change a man after they've gotten married. The only person you will ever have control over is yourself; therefore, it is self-deception to believe you can change another human being. See them as they are and decide if you can live with that person as is for the rest of your life. If you cannot, cut your losses before they get expensive. What cannot be worked out before the wedding is seldom worked out after exchanging vows. Take the time you need to be certain of the person you are marrying. You can't miss what you never had, but memories are difficult to erase, especially those filled with regret.

GETTING REAL

☞ What signs have you ignored in the past that you have regretted?

☞ What makes you ignore the signs? What impact does ignoring the signs have on your relationship as it progresses?

☞ What was your response to finding out the truth? Whom did you blame? Why?

☞ In what ways have you allowed mixed signals to mislead you before?

Number Six: Never Compromise Yourself

Let's talk about the deepest regret you can feel as a woman. That of investing your all, your everything, into someone who does not recognize your worth or treat you like the treasure you are. I'm talking about the regret of compromising your purity. No woman should ever have to sing the song "Will You Still Love Me Tomorrow?" Giving your body to someone who is not your husband is a huge mistake. Do away with the excuse that this is permissible because you are in a committed relationship. A man is not your husband until he is your husband. Consider this: How many other committed relationships have you had? Did you marry any of those men? There you have it. Consider if becoming physically involved with any of your former suitors had any bearing on the outcome of your relationship. Is it safe to say sexual intimacy only caused deeper pain when it was over? This is because sex is not just skin-deep. It is spirit-deep. Becoming one leaves an impression on our spirit that can never be erased.

Giving of yourself, of your body, can be compared to worship. The act of giving everything you are and everything you have should be reserved for the one who is willing to give his life for you. I have heard women say that sex gives them power over a man, but that is not scriptural.

The truth of the matter is you actually give up your power when you give in. The Word of God says that you become a servant to the one you yield your members to (Romans 6:16 KJV). No one should be able to hold that much power over you unless they are willing to pay the price in lifetime covenant. The cost of giving your body to one who is not committed to you in marriage is usually a lot higher than was anticipated. The pain of the remaining soul tie to one who has moved on can be debilitating.

For this reason God has set the standard of purity in place, not only to protect your heart but to keep you set apart for the one who will come deserving all of your love.

For those who have been engaged in numerous relationships, cynicism robs the heart of the hope that enabled it to once love fully. For every piece of yourself that you give away, the more difficult you will find it to reclaim the initial joy and fulfillment of love as God purposed it to be. Our hearts will be hedged with caution, distrust, and apprehension. Sometimes it can actually cause us to lose our discernment, making us unable to receive when the right thing finally comes along.

Oh, what peace we forfeit when we choose to walk against God's design, which was ordained for our protection. An important ingredient of maturity is to come to the understanding that responsible women take responsibility for not just their hearts, but their bodies and their spirits as well. It's in mastering the incredible balance of being secure in your sexuality and yet choosing to walk in purity that freedom and personal fulfillment are realized in the battle between the flesh and the spirit. This comes from having a full realization of your worth and a commitment to protecting those things considered valuable to God as well as yourself.

GETTING REAL

- In what ways have you compromised yourself in order to win a man's love? What was the outcome? What will you do differently next time?

- In what ways do you wrestle with your personal value? Why?

- What are the consequences of violating God's Word in the area of sex outside of marriage? How does this affect you emotionally?

- In the aftermath of rejection, what are your regrets when you've given your all to a man?

Number Seven: Don't Overstep Your Boundaries

When a man is ready to make a commitment, he moves heaven and earth to put his life in order to accommodate the woman he has decided is the best thing since sliced bread. Until then, he may enjoy spending time with you and having all the benefits of having a woman in his life without the responsibility associated with having a committed relationship. Therefore, don't behave like a significant other or girlfriend until he has made his intentions to be in a committed relationship with you crystal clear. If you have to guess, you are not in a relationship! A relationship is official when two parties have discussed moving forward together and mutually agreed to do so. Never leave this to assumption.

It has been said that a man will only do what a woman allows. If you allow him to continue on in a noncommittal state, he will take full advantage of all that you offer without ever committing more of himself to you or the relationship. Rutgers University did a study on why the trend on men committing had slowed to such an alarming rate. The men all said they did not feel they had to commit. They were already experiencing the full benefits of marriage without having to be married.

Women are more in control than they realize. It simply becomes an issue of what we choose to allow or disallow. When you act as a wife before you are a wife, chances are you will not become a wife. You have given a man nothing to aspire to. The old rule is still the same. Always leave him wanting more. It should be on his mind day and night how he can capture more of you, not how he can get you to back off or, worse yet, how he doesn't have to do more than he's doing or worry about you not being there. If you are "skimming" in a relationship, as I call it, admit that you are allowing this unacceptable behavior out of fear. The fear that if you let on that you want more from the relationship, he will flee. If that is true, believe me, he will be gone at some point anyway and you are merely putting off the inevitable. Value yourself enough not to allow another person to waste your time.

Time is a precious commodity to a woman, depending on what your lifetime goals are. If your life picture includes children, you have time parameters that cannot be ignored. That is not a lack of faith—that is reality. If you feel time is running out for some of the options you long for in life, I highly recommend making peace with that and count it all joy that in God's infinite wisdom He knew that might not be the best option for you, even though it was something you wanted. I always think on this Scripture when facing a moment like that: "He gave them their request, but sent leanness into their soul" (Psalm 106:15 NKJV). I thank Him for withholding anything from me that would place me in spiritual or even physical or emotional danger or famine. Remember that God knows best, and though we can make plans for our lives, His will prevails and His will is always best for us. But back to the point.

Whether your issue is time sensitive or not, don't allow anyone to waste your time or your emotional energy on a relationship that will not profit you emotionally or spiritually in the end. I realize that many hang on, praying that their man will someday wake up and smell the coffee. See the light or otherwise you will be sorely disappointed to find these long, drawn out relationships fading to black like a bad movie. What you must keep in mind is that you are the director. You need to call the shots, and when the scene lasts too long without any sign of resolve, it's time to yell "Cut!"

Let's discuss the famous "Let's be friends" line. Here is where smart women make foolish moves. When a man tells you this, it's his way of coasting while he checks out his options. In other words, he wants the benefit of relationship without the responsibility. He has not decided if you are it, which means you probably are not because men usually know this early in the game. He is still looking. And even though he is still looking, he does not want to give up the security and perks of having a woman in his life. Yet he does not want to get too deeply entrenched should he find what he is really looking for and have to extricate himself. He may just consider you a suitable stand-in and nothing more.

This is for you to know and not get an attitude about. Again, don't get mad; get smart. Treat him like a friend. However, his priority level should drop because you had other friends before he came along. He should be treated like all the rest of them. Which means he is not first in the pecking order. You are not available every time he calls. You do not drop everything to accept an invitation from him, because if you are truly friends he cannot take your time or your schedule for granted. Right?

This also means that you are free to explore other options. It would not be wise to sit and wait for him to change his mind, because he might not. If he does decide after perusing the scene that you are indeed a great catch, you can reconsider if you are still available then, but in the meantime move on.

Keep in mind that your time, your mind, your body, your presence, and your love add up to a valuable commodity! Anyone who cannot recognize that is not ready for prime-time TV. It is *their* loss, not yours. Consider merchandise at the store. Just because someone does not buy it does not mean that its value decreases. It's simply a matter of the right person coming along and recognizing what that particular piece of merchandise adds to them. And as you know, every garment doesn't look good on every body. A good fit is definitely required. And that goes both ways. So take good care of yourself. You belong to God, so carry yourself as the precious prize that you are, knowing that on the right day at the right time the right man will come along and choose you—yes, you—to be the star of his show. And all you have to do is show up and be who you are—graciously, of course.

GETTING REAL

∽ What has been the repetitive pattern in all of your relationships? What can you do differently to break this pattern?

∽ In what ways have you wasted time in your relationships in the past? Why? What was the outcome?

∽ Why is it important not to waste your time?

∽ What are God's expectations on how you spend your time?

Number Eight: Be Open to Wise Counsel

Once upon a time I had a friend…well, I still do, but we had to recover from a major setback due to the interruption of a man. She met this guy one day, fell head over heels in love with him, and lost her mind in the process. She didn't introduce him to friends or family until she sent out wedding invitations. She literally had disappeared into a black hole during their courtship and did not resurface until it was time to announce the upcoming nuptials. No one had a chance to meet him beforehand. Her explanation was simply this: "I just didn't want to have people asking me about another relationship that might not work out, so I decided to wait until I closed the deal." She closed the deal, all right, and then the mess hit the fan. All of the things she didn't know beforehand surfaced in her beloved. He was violent, abusive, unstable, couldn't keep a job—shall I go on? The marriage was a costly disaster for my dear friend, who found that getting out of the relationship was much harder than getting in.

This completely boggled my mind and my understanding. I attended the wedding, and he seemed very nice, but his family was a tad strange to me, and I wondered if my friend really got along with these people. I just did not see the connection. But, of course, any observations and input would have been a moot issue at this point. The deed had been done and she was going to have to live with it. And live with it she did for quite a while before the pressure of living unhappily finally took its toll and overruled her pride. One day she crumbled before me and spilled out all the gruesome details of what she had been enduring.

As the awful story unfolded, there were so many danger signs along the way I had to scratch my head at why these things had not been obvious to my dear friend. But as she described their romance, I began to understand it more clearly. He had done and said all the right things. Wined and dined her. Given her all the attention she had been so sorely lacking. She was distracted by the delirium of combustible chemistry and romance. After all, what would a starving dog do if he spotted a bone? You got that right, sister. Attack full on! Well, that's what she did. And now, as her marriage lay in shambles around her feet, she invited those near and dear to her to help pick up the pieces.

The moral of the story? Remain transparent and accountable to friends and family and don't ignore wise counsel, even if you don't like it. The Word of God talks about the importance of embracing wisdom. God dedicated an entire book to wisdom in Proverbs and encourages us to treat wisdom like a sister (Proverbs 7:4). If we do, long life, riches, and honor will be ours. The bottom line? If you want things to go well with you and your relationships, you have to use your head! Now is not the time to become so secretive you get lost in your own dark corner or so spiritual you are no earthly good. Relationships cannot be spiritualized. Though we are not of it, we still live in a cold, hard, natural world. The natural part of our existence does not go away. We simply add the spiritual dimension to our lives as we partner with God on a daily basis, thus adding the "super" element to our lives that ultimately should result in a supernatural lifestyle.

This means we must still deal with the fact that people in and out of church can have character issues that are not conducive to victorious relationships. Because God calls us to walk in wisdom, these are things we should consider before we enter into covenant, as it grieves the heart of God when we break covenant. So do your homework before you get in too deep. It is very dangerous to be swept away by pure emotion and chemistry.

The truth of the matter is that when we get caught up in the rapture of love, we are not interested in the fine print, warnings, or anything that could signal an end of the good feelings we are experiencing. This is why it's good to submit that man to others who are not clouded over in euphoria to check him out. If the marriage altar is where you ultimately want to land, remember, "Plans fail for lack of counsel, but with many advisers they succeed" (Proverbs 15:22).

Who should you seek counsel from? Proverbs 27:9 tells us that "the pleasantness of one's friend springs from his earnest counsel." Seek counsel from friends who earnestly want the best for you and are rooting for your happiness and well-being. That means don't consult with those who might be jealous, who say mean things out of their own pain or have shown you signs of not being in your corner before. To be perfectly honest, I would not submit a male friend to anyone who was not either in a victorious love relationship or living victoriously as a single. You should always seek counsel from those who are successfully doing what you would like to do. Otherwise, you might need to take the counsel with a grain of salt.

If the truth is being spoken in love, take it in no matter how hard it may be to hear. A hard decision now can save you from a world of heartache and lasting pain later. Remember, "The truth will set you free" (John 8:32). Sometimes it doesn't feel good, but, like medicine, truth is good for you. In this case, consider the truth preventative medicine. God never wanted us to have to learn things the hard way. This is why He gives us discernment. As we stay sensitive to His leading and the counsel of others, we choose the way that is best for us to take.

This brings me to the next point, which is that the counsel of God should absolutely be your foremost desire and should not be overlooked in this or any area of your life. James 1:5 says, "If any of you lacks wisdom, [she] should ask God, who gives generously to all without finding fault, and it will be given to [her]." Joshua 9 tells of the Gibeonites, a group of people who approached Joshua and the Israelites while they were claiming the Promised Land and deceived them into entering into a treaty of peace with them. Because no one sought the counsel of the Lord (Joshua 9:14), Joshua and the men of Israel didn't find out until later that these crafty people were actually enemies of Israel who lived close by. But now the Israelites were bound by an oath. How many women have found themselves caught up in whirlwind courtships, only to have the nightmare begin on the honeymoon night?

My most urgent advice is that you ask God to reveal the hidden things about the man you are considering before you get deeply involved. Don't even waste your time with someone who should not be considered seriously. Every man you meet is not a potential mate; they may be just a good friend or a bad distraction. God will open your eyes and make it clear if you really want to know the truth. Of course, when He reveals the inner workings of this man's heart to you, it is up to you to choose the path of wisdom after that.

Last, but certainly never least, are your parents. Might I caution you here urgently to never consider getting married without the blessing of your parents or someone who is in a place of authority in your life? That can be a married couple, mentor, or pastor. I have counseled far too many people on the brink of divorce. When I ask them what their parents thought of their mate, the answer is always the same. "Oh, they didn't like them. They didn't want me to marry this person." It never fails. Although you are an adult yourself, please understand that your parents know you. They've watched you develop over time and are probably more aware of who you are and what your needs are than you can imagine. They are looking for things you are not looking for, but the bottom line is they are not going to embrace someone they believe will break your heart.

Always ponder the source, but please at least consider what they have to say. No one ever turned out the worse for listening to good, solid counsel. At the end of the day your very life, peace, and happiness will depend on it. Counsel ignored before the wedding will only be sought in a counselor's office after the honeymoon. A wise woman asks questions before and regrets nothing later.

GETTING REAL

- Where are your blind spots when it comes to considering a potential love interest?

- What is your response to counsel when people offer it to you?

- Who are the members of your accountability circle? Are their lives representative of the type of life you would like to model?

- What happened the last time you ignored counsel? What did this teach you?

Number Nine: Maintain Your Femininity

Although sistahs are doing everything for themselves, the common consensus is still that none of them really want to be by themselves. So how does a woman balance her streak of necessary independence with being dependant enough to make a man feel needed in her world? To be or not to be needy—that is the question. The answer? Don't be needy to the point where a man is your oxygen, but be woman enough to make him feel like a man in your presence. I will remind you again that men fall in love with you based on the way they feel when they are around you. Therefore, make him feel like the king he longs to be in your eyes. A real woman does not feel the need to do what a man can do when a man is in her presence. There is no need to reiterate how powerful you are to a man. This is something they already know and are threatened by.

A woman can make or break a man. Take the story of Samson and Delilah (Judges 16). How does a strong man like that end up being lassoed, beaten down, and rendered helpless? Because some woman caused him to be so, that's why. It was to a woman that he revealed the secret of his strength, and it was by her hands that he fell. Poor guy didn't know what hit him. One minute he was reveling in the arms of this beautiful seductive woman; the next he was being carted away in chains, bound in a dungeon. He who had been feared by the masses was now ridiculed by all. Reduced to this by the wiles of not an army, but one woman.

Juxtapose this against the man found in Proverbs 31, whose wife was an amazing woman who empowered her man to be at his best at home and in the community at large. She was a blessing to him in every way, and he rose up along with his children to sing her praises. She made him look good and reaped the reward of having her house as well as her man and all their affairs in order.

Truly the difference between a defeated man and one who personifies man according to God's design is the woman who helps him build his world and complete his God-given assignment. This is the area where Satan wreaks the most havoc, because he knows a man and woman who stand united in their God-designed roles are two of the most powerful people on the face of the earth. They have the power to change nations. For this purpose he does his best to breed distrust and divisiveness between the sexes. His greatest strategy is to set man at odds with the thing he desires most next to God—a woman. Or at least to keep him in perpetual turmoil over her to the point of absolute frustration and even violence.

Men fear rejection more than women do, and they measure their success by how women respond to them. No man wants to be a failure in the eyes of his woman. This is why they respond so poorly to criticism or correction. This is why they refuse to ask for directions when in our presence! This should free you to stop being on the defensive with men. They are not the enemy. They want to be their best for you, but they need your help in order to pull it off.

Ladies, we don't need to add to their fears and confusion. We need to allay it. How do we do that? By being secure in who we are as women and celebrating exactly that. Many women have cited that it is hard to be a woman. I contend that it is only hard to be a woman if you are trying to be a man. Whether in the bedroom or the boardroom, you've got to walk in your own shoes. The shoes you've been given fit perfectly, so wear them well. Let's take stock of what we have that men don't. The ability to give life and nurture it. The ability to multitask. More mastery over vocal skills (this is huge). Ah, but the greatest gift of all is the gift of influence. While you are screaming about why men get to run everything, think again, my friend.

Don't tell me that influence is not more powerful than authority. Yes, man has been given authority by God, but He gave women something far more powerful—the gift of influence. It was a woman who influenced a man to give up everything he possessed with one bite of fruit (Genesis 3:6). Wars have been fought over women. Nations have tumbled because of women. Because his heart beat a little faster at a glance from her, his stomach flipped, over when she smiled, and he couldn't get her out of his mind, a man will go all out. We have lost the art of femininity in today's society. (Check out my book *The Power of Being a Woman* for more on this.) The war between the sexes has turned into a vicious contest, with women advancing and men digging in their heels, resisting with all their might. Time-out!

How do we get the romance and the wonder for one another back? By celebrating the way God made us and acknowledging the gifts He has placed in us both. He gave man the incredible capacity for loyalty and the deep kind of love that protects and covers a woman to his dying breath. The amazing ability to separate logic from emotion and problem solve. To see things in black and white and calmly proceed to bring order to chaos. They are fixers. Stabilizers. They were created for dominion and the suppression of evil. We bring fruitfulness to their world and the ability to build and rule kingdoms. We add beauty and discernment to their world. We being an amazing bundle of contradictions add the color to their black and white. We balance one another. We complement one another. We complete one another. How awesome is that?

If you could just wrap your head around what you bring to a man's world, perhaps it would free you to be more gracious and less suspicious. Less anxious to rule and more inclined to inspire. This is when we are liberated to walk in the very nature of God, who is so gracious because He rests in the knowledge that He is God whether we ever accept Him as such or not. He will not be robbed or devalued if we don't see or acknowledge how amazing He is. He will still be God even if we don't submit our lives to Him. Nothing and no one takes away from who He is and who He always will be. This should be your mind-set. You have nothing to prove. You are beautiful. Intelligent. Fruitful. Nurturing. *A good thing.* Shall I go on or do you finally get the picture? Who you are is who you've always been whether anyone ever recognizes it or not! Begin to own that woman that you look at in the mirror and understand that no one can diminish the greatness you harbor within but yourself.

The lie that this is a man's world has women rebelling while citing all the horrible things that men do to dominate women. Those who live in fear will always rule with far more strength than is required. Why be surprised by that? Choose to understand it instead. I'm reminded of a line in the movie *The Stepford Wives.* Mike, the ringleader of the men who were bent on turning their wives into robots, said, "When women decided to become men, men decided to become gods." Whew! That is deep. People always try to contain what they fear. Remember that.

So how do we disarm the enemy? By taking the fear factor out of the relationship. By being a partner, a supporter, and a safe confidante. By causing his heart to trust in you, like the woman in Proverbs 31. Stop fighting the whole submission thing and come to the place of understanding that submission is not about being a doormat. It is the vehicle for putting yourself in the position to be blessed. What happens when you submit to your boss at work and do what you've been asked to do? You get rewarded with pay, correct? What happens when you submit to the law and stop at a red light? You are saved the devastation of being hit by oncoming traffic, right? Laws are put in place for our safety. Rules are set in place to create order. Order and safety create an environment for people to flourish and be blessed. And that is all God wants for all of us. But if the devil can keep confusion going, he will.

Just so this whole submission thing gets put in perspective, the Bible states that wives should submit to their own husbands (Ephesians 5:22). Not anyone else's—their own. Your boyfriend is not your husband; however, if you cannot exhibit a team-player attitude during the courtship phase, it is going to be difficult to just slip into automatic submission when you become a wife. Submission is nothing more than cooperating with those who are on your team. This is why the blanket clause in the Word of God is that we all should submit to one another (Ephesians 5:21). The principle at work here is go with the one who is gifted in what you are trying to accomplish. Honor one another and work together. Life is not a contest; it is a journey that requires help along the way. We are all in this thing together, so cut each other some slack.

One last thought on this matter for when you cross over the threshold of singleness into marriage. Ladies, you do your husband a serious disservice if you decide that you are the one who knows best in the relationship and you are not going to submit to his leadership. You put him in the position to reap God's displeasure, which seriously hinders him from being blessed. This has a trickle-down effect to you, and in the end you rob yourself.

Remember poor Adam in the Garden of Eden? Though Eve reaped her own consequences for her afternoon snack, Adam was chastised for listening to her. After that he had to work hard in the fields to care for himself and his family. Most men have a fear of not being productive. A man's field or workplace is very much the place that affirms his manhood. His failure or success in the marketplace is a large part of what defines him as he struggles to prove his worth to his woman. You put him in the position to struggle even more if you are not empowering him to fulfill his mandate from God to cover you and be responsible for the direction you move in as a couple.

This does not mean that you do not get to have your say. You do. If you do things the right way, your man will not just invite but honor your opinions and thoughts on things, but it must begin with how you position yourself and the posture you take toward him. Walk in the confidence that you are in that man's life as a helpmeet for him. The confidence that you are needed by him should make you want to gently and graciously give your opinion—minus attitude. And remember that at the end of the day if he is not the man you think he needs to be, then you must examine your part in that calculation because your presence in his life is supposed to make him a better man. So get on your job, girlfriend! Practice begins now with the men who are friends and brothers in your life. Celebrate them. Celebrate yourself. And celebrate the difference you make in one another's lives.

GETTING REAL

- What are the things that you celebrate most about being a woman?

- What are your greatest struggles with being a woman?

- What is your view of submission? How has this hurt you/ helped you in various situations such as work and relationships?

- In what ways can you add to a man's life?

Number Ten: Be Patient

Timing is everything. For everything there is a season. A time to connect. A time to let things simmer. A time to close the deal. In each of these phases you must be careful not to try to make things happen. Be available to the possibilities but don't push! Women have become so aggressive it's hard to separate the appropriate from the inappropriate, and yet there is a thin line between being proactive and too forward.

If we truly trust that God reigns over our destiny, then a question begs to be asked: Isn't He Lord over everything that occurs in our life, including bringing the right man into our world? As you, like Ruth, go about the business of living and flourishing where you have been planted, can't your steps be ordered of the Lord just as He has promised so you, like Ruth, happen upon that X that marks the spot in the Spirit for that not-so-much-by-chance meeting with Mr. Right? But of course! And even when you see him checking you out, talk to yourself, girl, and say, "Patience, patience...take it slow now." Sit back and let him come to you. If you're with a group of women, separate yourself from the crowd and smile nicely so he knows it's safe to approach. Most men don't like approaching a group of women and becoming a victim of their perusal when they are trying to get the attention of one of them. Remember, they fear rejection.

Go ahead. Have wonderful, light conversation. Be interested but do not initiate the next step. If he wants to pursue you, he will ask for a way to contact you. "Patience, patience." He gives you his card and you give him yours...Now the waiting game begins. "Patience, patience." Do not jump at the phone every time it rings, girl. Simmer down! If he hasn't called by day two, don't you call him. It's his job to initiate contact. He is the hunter; you are the game. "But, Michelle, what if he lost my number!" Well, if it is to be and your steps are ordered of the Lord, you will run into him again. Otherwise, he should have taken better care of your card if it was important to him.

Let me tell you a little story to show you what I mean. I met a man at a function once. He handed me his business card and asked me to call him. By the time I recovered he was gone. A woman seated at the table with me turned to me and said, "Give me one of your cards." "Why, I just gave you one," I answered. She said, "I am going to give him your card because I know you won't call him. I've read your books!" I laughed and gave her the card, which she then gave to him, advising him to call me. I did not hear from him for two days. On the third day I received a call from the assistant of the man who had purchased the table at the function I attended. She informed me that this man had called their offices frantically trying to find me because he had lost my card! I gave her permission to pass my number on to him. He promptly called and invited me out to an amazing dinner. Again I will say, "Patience, patience." If that man really wants to get to know you, he will track you down, girlfriend. And that is what you want.

So you go out. You have a wonderful time. You like him. He likes you. "Patience, patience." Watch and wait. Don't get too happy yet. Let's see if he is consistent. My mentor Bunny Wilson always reminds me that "patience is the tool that uncovers deceit." This is where you coast and see where you end up. Now is not the time to start planning wedding colors and naming your children. Let's see if he can last past the microwave express stage. If he's calling constantly, you must pace him so he doesn't burn himself out. You do not want him to start habits he cannot maintain. He will only become overwhelmed and fizzle out because he can't keep up and feels guilty about it.

So now he passes the test. He's proven that he is intentional and consistent. "Patience, patience." There will come a time when he might draw back in fear if he thinks he's getting in too deep. Should this occur, let him go and wait, but not on him. Wait on the Lord to reveal what's next or deal with him or both. Wait. The man must do the business of stepping up to the plate and closing the deal. You can ask questions on what his intentions are if he is attempting to monopolize all of your time without voicing his intentions. You can't afford to give your time or yourself away without knowing what you are investing in and/or if you will have a return on your investment.

Ask but don't push. Just let him know that you feel vulnerable toward him and you need to know if your heart is safe. Do not express feelings of love before him! Remember, you were created to be a receiver. You were created to respond to his love. Allow him to do the calling until he makes it clear that you are in an exclusive relationship and then you should still keep it down. Ever notice about the time you get comfortable with calling he begins to behave strangely? If you want to be taken for granted, all you have to do is become too aggressive or too available. In order to maintain your value, be available but not easy access.

This also means no overdoing it on gifts, etc. We are wired to give and nurture, but there is a time for everything. This area can make a guy uncomfortable unless he is a player, and then he will just take advantage of you. A nice guy might feel he now has to reciprocate and either match or top what you have done. This is too much work for him. Unless you are secure in your relation-ship and he has shown displays of affection with impromptu gifts and such, hold back on this one. The greatest gift you can ever give him is yourself. As long as you nurture the art of being a great listener and a fun and inspiring woman to be around, he will feel he has all the gifts he needs wrapped up in you.

In the world of business, the rule of thumb is the person who speaks first loses the deal. This is important to remember. Keep the declarations of love to yourself until he has made his intentions clear. Now, here is the one caveat to this whole principle. I am not giving you license to have patience forever. I am not advocating the looooong drawn out relationship that takes years to resolve. First of all, it will be hard to maintain walking in purity, and you will run into other problems that will compromise your relationship. I am talking about having patience in the process of the time it takes to meet, form a friendship, and then move on to intentional courtship. A man knows in his spirit what he wants from you relatively early in the relationship, if not at first sight. From every discussion with a man that I've had on this subject, most knew right away. So there is no excuse for the long drawn out relationship where he still can't make up his mind after two years what he wants to do with you. He knows; he just doesn't want to do it with you. The truth will set you free to be found by someone else who sees your value. Next!

Though this is one of the hardest things to master, it is also the key to living and loving from a position of power. We were not created to be desperate by any stretch of the imagination. God calls us to master our hearts, our lives, our everything. Patience is a sign that puts others on notice that you know your worth. When you know your worth, you don't have to sell yourself. You walk in the expectancy that others see and understand your value. Too bad for them if they don't. As wisdom teacher Mike Murdock says and I agree, "You need to go where you are celebrated and not just tolerated." Patience waits for the dust of euphoria to settle, and then carefully assesses the lay of the land to see if this is the place it would like to remain. Not based on first impressions, but on the scenery over time. Patience helps you to own yourself and not make moves you may regret later. Sometimes the shame is greater than the pain of a love gone wrong when you realize you did not conduct yourself with wisdom. So hold your breath and exhale slowly. Never make a decision out of fear, anger, or passion. Wait on the Lord. He will always make the way clear.

You haven't been this far to even try any of this out? "Patience, patience." Your day will come. Not a day late, or a moment out of time. And trust me. It will be sooo worth the wait.

GETTING REAL

   In what ways have you been impatient in your past relationships? What was the outcome?

   What fuels your impatience? What do you fear losing? What would allay your fears?

   How important is being in control to you?

   What makes you feel most out of control? How does God factor into the equation when you feel this way?

The heart of the wise inclines to the right,

but the heart of the fool to the left

(Ecclesiastes 10:2).

SOLOMON,
a man of unsurpassed wisdom,
commenting on true wisdom.

Giving up and caving in

Just thinking out loud...

She was a single girl, young and impressionable when she found herself thrust into the midst of other women all vying for the attention of one man. As others around her used all their wiles to capture his heart, she stayed true to herself. Perhaps he noticed her authenticity because in the end she was chosen. She won the favor of all around her with her quiet beauty and godly countenance. Later, when the lives of her people were being threatened, it was she who served her husband and won his support, defeating her enemy quietly. Not only was the safety of her people secured, the heart of her husband safely trusted in her. Esther finished well. (Look again at Esther's story in the book of Esther.)

He was single. A long way from home with abuse in his past. He had suffered at the hands of those who should have been his greatest allies—his brothers. Yet in the midst of a foreign society, with very different morals and a lifestyle that opposed all he had been taught to revere, he stood firm. In the face of overwhelming temptation he maintained his purity. When wrongly accused by a scorned woman, he did not grow defensive or bitter through the harsh injustice he suffered. He kept the faith and in the end his chance came. He was promoted far above his expectations and blessed with a wife and two beautiful sons. He rose up to save his nation and died with dignity in the presence of his loved ones, passing on blessings to the next generation. Joseph finished well. (See Genesis chapters 37–50.)

She had only been married for seven years when her husband died. She never remarried. Instead, she chose to spend her time seeking God and serving His people in the temple. Her greatest desire was to see the Messiah, the One who would deliver her people from their suffering. So she gave herself to fasting and prayer daily, trusting that God would deliver the promise in her lifetime. And then one day there they were, this young couple standing in the temple. The mother was holding the most incredible baby boy in her arms, and she knew He was the Chosen One. She felt as if her journey was finally completed. She had waited more than 70 years to witness this sight. As she prophesied over the child, her joy was full and she went her way praising God and sharing the good news with others. Anna finished well. (See Luke 2:36-38.)

He was thirtyish, passionate, with a lot of love to give. Some were drawn to His gentleness. Some thought that He was weird while others found Him charismatic. He was misunderstood, rejected, and betrayed, and yet He never lost hope, never stopped loving, and when asked to lay down His life for those who treated Him so badly, He gladly did so. He stayed focused on the goal, paying the dowry to redeem His bride. He never complained about the cost. He didn't try to defend Himself when wrongly accused. He never grew bitter; He was gracious to the end. And He is still waiting to claim His bride. In spite of how long He has waited, He has remained faithful. Jesus finished well. (See John 14:1-3.)

Throughout the Bible, men and women found themselves in situations comparable to our contemporary circumstances. We can all relate to feeling as if we were in an unending beauty contest when it comes to being chosen by a man. Or perhaps we experienced a brief respite of happiness with someone, only to have them taken away prematurely through death or choosing to depart. Maybe we've found ourselves in conditions that are not of our choosing, where we question our choices or how we ended up where we are. Perhaps we are dealing with the jealousy of loved ones or coworkers and feeling as if we will break under their unnecessary barbs and attitudes.

The pressure of life can weigh heavy on us when we feel as if we have to go it alone...when even those who are walking with us don't really get us or our vision. It can be a lonely place, and yet our examples show us that we don't have to give up, slow down, or grow weary of cultivating and maintaining a rich single life. It really is about finishing well. Whether our desires or expectations are met or not, we get to choose the ending to our personal stories. We can edit in victory or failure, perseverance or resignation, overcoming or survival. Every day of our lives we get to choose life or death and make decisions that invite blessing or cursing into our lives. Single or married, the struggle is the same—to live a life that brings pleasure to the heart of God and peace, joy, and fulfillment to ourselves and all we encounter. No matter what our circumstances, whether it changes or not, we want to finish gracefully, finish stylishly, finish well.

LET'S STAY STRONG TO THE END

ℂ List five things that would make life more perfect for you.

ℂ What things on the list are wants versus needs? What must you have? What could you live—and live well—without?

ℂ How would you live your life if you never got what was on your list?

ℂ What decisions can you make about your life in order to finish well?

Solution: Finish well

Let's face it. Most things in life don't happen when we want them to, how we want them to, or where and with whom we want them to. Most people have a story about the one that got away. Should circumstances rule our joy factor or our productivity? I think not! The challenge to flourish in spite of which pot we get planted in offers us an exciting opportunity to become outstanding citizens of the world and leave a mark of excellence whether we ever get married or not.

I passionately believe that the secret to successful single living is truly to live every day as if you were never going to get married. How much freer would you be with the absence of desperation or the perpetual timekeeper on the mantel of your heart tick, tick, ticking away? You could actually meet a nice guy and not worry about whether he is a potential husband or not. You could simply enjoy his company for what it's worth. You would learn to live in the moment and make each of them rich, inspiring ones. You would open yourself to joy! Because we do not know the future, we must decide how we are going to face our tomorrows. Will we run and not grow weary, walk and not faint? Or will we go splat because we're not being served the dish we want right now? Or, worse yet, crawl across the finish line of life worse

for wear because the track went somewhere we never anticipated? May I encourage you to decide to finish well no matter
what your status is in life? This is something that you can control
simply by renewing your attitude.

When the apostle Paul, who, by the way, was very single, was
writing a letter to one of his mentees and colaborers, Timothy,
he gave him some words of encouragement that I think we could
all profit from in our single journey.

First, he told Timothy, who was feeling quite alone at the
time, to keep his head in all situations (2 Timothy 1:6-7). Your
heart may deceive you at times. Depending on how hungry you
are for the things that you desire, its voice might scream louder
than the still, small voice that will caution you to take a second
look at your choice. Keep your head, ladies. Don't just keep it;
use it. As the saying goes, if it walks like a duck, and quacks like
a duck, it's probably a duck! Emotions will never be accurate
indicators of what we need to do, therefore be still, listen to the
voice of God, and follow His instructions. Don't allow yourself
to be pushed over the edge by anger, fear, or even passion. These
are filters that usually screen reason and wisdom from presenting
their side of the argument in the war for your flesh. By now you
know that all it takes is one wrong move to start an avalanche of
occurrences that can increase our pain and take us further away
from all that we've been longing for.

Next, Paul says, endure hardship (2 Timothy 1:8). Let's face
it. Life can be rough whether you are married or single. When
life stinks just flip the fertilizer, my friend. What doesn't kill you
should make you stronger, not worse than you were. Know that
God allows tests and trials to prune us and purge away all the
things that are not conducive to showcasing the gifts He has
given you in their best light. Life and all its various changes and

seasons has a way of birthing maturity, grace, and strength in us if we let it. Use the pain in hardship to mold you into a stronger person. Let the trying of your faith work out patience in you. Determine to grow from your experiences and become more fruitful and productive because of what you learned in the midst of the struggle. If you think single life is hard, wait until you get married and have to persevere through trials times two! Now is the time to develop character that can only add richness to your marital experience.

Paul tells Timothy to do the work of an evangelist (2 Timothy 4:5). Well, you might not be an evangelist, but you are an ambassador for God no matter what your profession or life path. You are a living, walking representative of God. Work it out. Work it out by being the best you that you can be on a daily basis. Represent God well by living your life well. Do the work it takes to excel in every area of your life.

First, do the work spiritually. Take the time for devotion. Center yourself. Read the Word and fill yourself with not just wisdom but comfort, strength, and encouragement for each day. Pray. Keep your connection to God strong. This will carry you when there are no arms to hold you. Worship. Learn to celebrate God's goodness in your life and revel in the joy that this sort of intimacy with your Creator brings. Fellowship with others. Get involved at church or in some organization where you have the opportunity to serve others. Practice being a part of family and community.

Do the work physically. You get one body. Take care of it. If you don't like exercise, find something to do to keep your body strong. Watch your diet. Do this as unto the Lord. Not only is your body the place where your soul lives, it is the temple of the Holy Spirit. When you invite guests to your home, don't you want it to look its best? Well, the Holy Spirit has come to visit and take up residence inside of you. Do the work to make Him enjoy His stay. In order to look your best you must feel your best, so take the time to nurture the body that God gave you so that it works for you and not against you.

Do the work professionally. Work as if you are working for the Lord Himself. Go the extra mile. Strive to be excellent. Knowing that you've done your best is a fulfilling feeling. Remember that it's not just about you. You represent the Lord in the marketplace, as well as the body of Christ. Make us look good. Represent well. Do the work it takes to go to the next level. Promotion doesn't just happen; it is earned. Be diligent. Be focused. Work joyfully. God gives us all the power to get wealth, but you've got to do the work in order to tap into the abundance that awaits you. Remember, He is glorified when you succeed, but you've got to do the work. Success happens when opportunity meets preparation. Success is maintained by diligence and focus. Do the work.

Do the work emotionally. No one else can set you free. Only you can partner with God to be emotionally free, whole, and open to give and receive love. Clear your decks. Get rid of the baggage. Rinse off your heart and give it permission to have a fresh start. To hope like you never have before. To love as if you've never been hurt. You get to decide your emotional destiny by adjusting your responses to what you have experienced in the past. Get counseling if you need to. Hold yourself accountable to someone you can trust to tell you the truth in love. Do whatever you have to do but...do the work. Get real. Get honest about where you've been and how you feel. Confess, repent if you need to, but come clean. Hand over all that you are harboring to God and allow Him to wash you with all the tears you've cried before. Then dare to begin again.

Do the work relationally. Take the time to listen and really hear. Take the time to respond not out of your wants, but out of the other person's need. Practice the regimen of true love, kindness, patience, bearing all things, and hoping for even better. Uh-huh, you know what I'm talking about. I'm talking about stretching. Doing the work...weeping with those who weep. Bearing the infirmities of the weak. Dying to self. Considering others above yourself. Submitting one to the other. Sounds like a lot of work, doesn't it? But I thought you wanted to be married? These character traits don't happen overnight. They come from a lifetime of practice. Now is the perfect time to begin.

If you don't do the work now, you will do the work later, and the labor might be more intensive because another person will be involved. Learn to master these skills and be a gift to the one God presents you to.

In the same breath, Paul advises Timothy to fulfill his ministry (2 Timothy 4:5). Ministry is not just standing on a platform preaching. Ministry is touching people wherever you're placed by God. Joining the coffee klatch at work to complain about the unavailability of good men and how miserable it is to be single is not ministry, and it certainly doesn't separate you from the rest of the world. But possessing genuine joy as a single person and rejoicing in your love affair with the Lover of your soul gives you a powerful platform to share that same peace and joy with others who are struggling for validation and affirmation. Step out of yourself. Sense and respond to the needs around you. Feel the fulfillment that comes from doing what you were created to do every day—be a light. A beacon of hope. The reason that someone feels better. Be someone who tries harder. Dares to excercise their faith. Doesn't give up. After all, that is why you are really here, and you don't need to be married to do any of these.

Sometimes it will be a fight to keep your head above water. To stay above the peer pressure. The biological clock pressure. The hormonal pressure. The media pressure. Even the church pressure that says "You've got to get married now. You're nothing if you don't have someone. Your best years are passing you by." You have to cast down all those lies and silence the voices without and within that try to make you believe that you are unable to live your best life right now. Fight for your joy. Fight the good fight it takes to overcome negative mind-sets and low self-esteem, and don't settle for less than God's best for you. Fight to stay strong, to stay pure, to remain steadfast on the journey. You are going to have to fight to finish well. The enemy of your soul will not just hand the victory over to you on a silver platter. Like an Olympic medalist, you will have to use everything you have to move forward and claim the ultimate prize before reaching eternity, which is a life well lived. Things worth having never come easy. Fight to keep hope alive.

God's timing for your life demands that you keep the faith in order to finish well. He knows the plans He has for you. Unfortunately, you don't have all the details. I recall moping because I thought everyone had forgotten my birthday one year when I was in school. Little did I know they were planning an incredible surprise party for me. I became more surly as the day went on. Imagine my embarrassment when in spite of my bad attitude all day the celebration was unleashed. Can you imagine how we look to God as we go kicking and screaming through life, completely unaware of all the wonderful blessings He has stored up for us? Keep the faith. Trust His timing, and know it will be soooo worth the wait. How we wait is up to us. We can either sit down on life, cross our legs, and wait...and wait...or we can get busy serving God and man until He reveals His plans and manifests them in accordance with His perfect plan for us.

Decide now that you are going to finish the course. Paul was able to proudly proclaim that he felt he had done everything he had been put here to do (1 Timothy 4:7). I find it interesting that this same man felt that it was better to be single than married. He died a single man, and yet there was joy, peace, and contentment that resonated throughout his letters to the church as he shared his passion for the gospel with them. He was just as passionate about living a holy life and being a force to be reckoned with to the world at large. This totally consumed his life, and I just picture him folding his hands across his chest at the end of the day, totally satisfied that he had accomplished something of import for God.

When you leave this earth, no one is going to comment on your mate. They are going to comment on whatever legacy of works you left behind. Determine now to leave a profound mark on the lives of all you encounter. Finishing your course is not just rounding the bend and finishing the journey. It's about finishing the course that God wanted you to learn as well. Complete the lessons and determine to get an "A" on the paper of your life. Those who don't surrender are destined to get an "Incomplete" on their paper because the greatest things you can learn in life are simply: God loves you and He has a plan for your life. That plan includes His best for you, and His timing is always perfect. Whether you ever marry or not, God has fulfillment in store for you—if you choose to embrace it. The question is not when will you get married. It is how will you spend yout time right now?

If you were told you only had a week to live, would marriage be on your list of priorities? Dare to have a fabulous journey enjoying the scenery more than desperately looking for any set destination. You will arrive soon enough, and oh the sights you will miss along the way if you don't take the time to admire and appreciate all that God has placed on your path. Tomorrow is not promised, so make today a full-blown adventure. Live it with all the gusto you can muster and learn your lessons well. When all is said and done, you, like Paul, will look back on a rich, full existence, breathe deeply, and give praise to God for an incredible life that did not depend on anyone else to complete it, though they certainly added a measure of joy to what was already there. And that, my sister, is called truly arriving.

GETTING REAL

- In what ways have you allowed your emotions to lead your decisions? What was the outcome?

- What areas of your life do you need to work on? How will you apply yourself to gaining discipline in these areas?

- What is the greatest area of struggle for you in the area of faith? How can you strengthen yourself in this area?

- What lesson do you feel God wants you to learn right now? How will this affect your life when you finally absorb it?

- How will you fulfill your ministry on a daily basis?

I have fought the good fight,

I have finished the race,

I have kept the faith (2 Timothy 4:7).

PAUL,
reflecting on what was truly important.

More Encouraging Books
by Michelle McKinney Hammond

101 Ways to Get and Keep His Attention
Getting Smart About Life, Love, and Men
How to Be Found by the Man You've Been Looking For
How to Get Past Disappointment
The Power of Being a Woman
Right Attitudes for Right Living
A Sassy Girl's Guide to Loving God
Sassy, Single, and Satisfied
Sassy, Single, and Satisfied Devotional
Secrets of an Irresistible Woman
What to Do Until Love Finds You
Why Do I Say "Yes" When I Need to Say "No"?
A Woman's Gotta Do What a Woman's Gotta Do

To learn more about books
by Michelle McKinney Hammond
and to read sample chapters, log on to:

www.HarvestHousePublishers.com

HARVEST HOUSE PUBLISHERS
EUGENE, OREGON

What Are You Looking For?

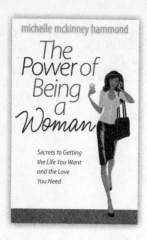

michelle mckinney hammond

The Power of Being a Woman

Secrets to Getting the Life You Want and the Love You Need

Romance? Healthy relationships? Success? Bestselling author and businesswoman Michelle McKinney Hammond can help. After exploring the positive attributes God gives to you as a woman, Michelle goes on to help you discover your own unique gifts and talents. With this firm foundation, she reveals how you can move forward confidently, using your new understanding and skills to

- influence rather than challenge
- master the balance between your personal and professional life
- experience harmony and passion in love
- effectively achieve your goals
- move mountains with your faith

Enthusiastic, outspoken, and entertaining, Michelle lives what she teaches. Let her help you experience the vibrant life God planned for you!

> *"[Michelle] calls a truce between the genders with her biblically based perspective on the art of being a woman."*
> TODAY'S CHRISTIAN WOMAN

For more information on Michelle McKinney Hammond
Log on to www.MichelleHammond.com
For booking information click on the booking tab at
www.MichelleHammond.com

Twitter: @mckinneyhammond
Facebook: Michelle-McKinney-Hammond
YouTube: heartwingmin